The Posture of Victory: Finding True Peace Amidst Our Everyday Battles

A Six-Week Study Based on Psalm 63

Theresa M. Miller

M⊕ Zion Ridge Press
Books Off the Beaten Path

www.MtZionRidgePress.com

Mt Zion Ridge Press LLC
295 Gum Springs Rd, NW
Georgetown, TN 37366
https://www.mtzionridgepress.com

ISBN 13: 978-1-962862-79-0
Published in the United States of America
Publication Date: July 1, 2025
Copyright: © 2025 Theresa Miller

Editor-In-Chief: Michelle Levigne
Executive Editor: Tamera Lynn Kraft
Cover art design by Tamera Lynn Kraft
Cover Art Copyright by Mt Zion Ridge Press LLC © 2025

Unless otherwise indicated, Scripture quotations are from The ESV® Bible (The Holy Bible, English Standard Version®), copyright © 2001 by Crossway, a publishing ministry of Good News
Publishers. Used by permission. All rights reserved.
Scripture quotations marked (NIV) are taken from the Holy Bible, New International Version®, NIV®. Copyright © 1973, 1978, 1984, 2011 by Biblica, Inc.™ Used by permission of Zondervan. All rights reserved.
Scripture quotations marked KJV from The Authorized (King James) Version. Rights in the Authorized Version in the United Kingdom are vested in the Crown. Reproduced by permission of the Crown's patentee, Cambridge University Press.

Table of Contents

Praise for the Posture of Victory   1
Introduction   3
Definitions   9
Psalm 63   11

Week One: Humbly Acknowledge God   13
Day One   14
Devotional: True Confidence
Day Two   17
Acknowledging Who God is, *"Oh, God…"*
Commentary, Part One:
Day Three   21
Soak, Scripture, and Scribble: *Our Confession*
Day Four   24
Acknowledging Who God is, *"My God…"*
Commentary, Part Two:
Day Five   27
Ponder and Personalized Practice: God's Presence in the
Wilderness
Scripture Informed Revelation   29

Week Two: Earnestly Seek God's Presence   31
Day One   32
Devotional: When Fear and Doubt Lurk
Day Two   35
Understanding Our Need for God, *Thirst*
Commentary, Part One:
Day Three   38
Soak, Scripture, and Scribble: *Seek*
Day Four   41
Understanding Our Need for God, *Longing*
Commentary, Part Two:

Day Five   44
Ponder and Personalized Practice: Seeking God in the Wilderness
Scripture Informed Revelation   46

Week Three: Remember God's Power and Glory   **47**
Day One   48
Devotional: Replacing Lies with Truth
Day Two   51
Cultivating a Desire for God, *Remembering*
Commentary, Part One:
Day Three   54
Soak, Scripture, and Scribble: *Promises*, Recognizing God's Faithfulness
Day Four   56
Cultivating a Desire for God, *Meditating*
Commentary, Part Two:
Day Five   59
Ponder and Personalized Practice: Getting Radical in the Wilderness
Scripture Informed Revelation   61

Week Four: Praise God No Matter the Circumstance   **63**
Day One   64
Devotional: Praise as a Pleasing Sacrifice
Day Two   67
Cultivating a Heart of Praise, *The Work of Our Whole Lives*
Commentary, Part One:
Day Three   71
Soak, Scripture, and Scribble: *Gratitude*
Day Four   74
Cultivating a Heart of Praise, *Our Response*
Commentary, Part Two:
Day Five   78
Ponder and Personalized Practice: Genuine Praise in the Wilderness
Scripture Informed Revelation   81

Week Five: Cleave to God As Though Your Strength Depends on It   **83**

Day One 84
Devotional: Living Boldly in Christ
Day Two 87
Learning to Depend Fully on God, *What It Means to Cleave*
Commentary, Part One:
Day Three 91
Soak, Scripture, and Scribble: *Under the Shadow*
Day Four 94
Learning to Depend Fully on God, *Upheld by God's Power*
Commentary, Part Two:
Day Five 97
Ponder and Personalized Practice: Strength Through The Wilderness
Scripture Informed Revelation 99

Week Six: Confidently Proclaim Victory **101**
Day One 102
Devotional: Defeat Is a Feeling
Day Two 104
Breaking Generational Cycles, *Anointing*
Commentary, Part One:
Day Three `109
Soak, Scripture, and Scribble: Crowns of Victory
Day Four 112
Breaking Generational Cycles, *How Liars Are Silenced*
Commentary, Part Two:
Day Five 116
Ponder and Personalized Practice: Victory through the Wilderness
Scripture Informed Revelation 119

Conclusion **121**
Appendices **123**
Acknowledgments **126**
About the Author **127**

Praise for the Posture of Victory

There's nothing more frustrating than knowing Christ has enabled us to walk in victory, yet we keep stumbling in defeat. That's why I'm grateful for this Bible study. If victory in Christ is your "want to," then these pages are your "how-to." Guided by the wisdom of Psalm 63, you'll learn how to adjust the posture of your heart, seek the strength of your Savior, and persevere in praise and prayer so you can stop wishing for victory in Christ and begin walking in it.

—**Alicia Bruxvoort,** *author, speaker, abundant life-seeker*
Proverbs 31 Writing team

The Posture of Victory is a refreshing and heartfelt guide for anyone longing to experience God's presence more deeply. Through her relatable stories and profound reflections on Psalm 63, Theresa M. Miller invites us to rediscover the joy and strength that come from leaning on God in life's wilderness moments. This six-week journey is not just a study; it's a heart-to-heart conversation that meets you where you are and gently points you back to the One who offers true peace. You'll find encouragement, practical steps, and the kind of spiritual nourishment that leaves you saying, 'I'm so glad I didn't walk this road alone.' A crucial study for anyone ready to embrace God's victory in their everyday battles!

—*Jennifer J. Camp*
author of **Breathing Eden:**
Conversations with God on Light, Fresh Air, and New Things

The Posture of Victory renewed my confidence in God's prosperous plan for my life. It spoke straight to my soul. Directly into the spaces that have felt hindered by fear. Callings that felt threatened by circumstances and opinions of the world. Desires and dreams that seem detoured by struggle and feelings of disappointment and defeat. Theresa stands solid on scripture to remind us that, though the enemy is working to keep us from where God is guiding us, our Supreme God has the final say. This well-written bible study will broaden your awareness of who God is, deepen your understanding of what he says, and show you how to walk confidently in your calling with his help and strength. I want everyone to soak in this study to equip us all to advance God's kingdom and live out our purposes, leading to a more joyful, peaceful life of fruitfulness and fulfillment.

—*Keri Eichberger*
author of **Win Over Worry:**
Conquer What Shakes You and Soar With the One Who Overcomes

The Posture of Victory offers a fresh, transformative approach to Psalm 63, guiding readers to apply David's postures of faith in their own lives. Miller's clear guidance and unique insights make this study practical and deeply impactful for anyone seeking to grow closer to God."

—**Dr. Gladys Childs**
author of **Busting Barriers:**
Overcome Emptiness & Unleash Fruitful Living

In The Posture of Victory: Finding True Peace Amidst Our Everyday Battles, Theresa shows us how to do battle like David did in Psalm 63, and it begins with our posture. The significance of our mindset or posture is evident in the Scriptures, which is what much of my doctoral work focused on. Our posture is not just an attitude in a vacuum — it impacts our entire life. Theresa helps the reader recognize how posture impacts our peace and empathizes with her reader as one who has experienced recurring defeat yet found the secret to walking in victory. Tucked in the Scriptures is our answer. This victory in Christ is not merely anecdotal, but a certainty for those willing to believe and walk in the victory Christ achieved on the cross.

—**Denise Pass, PhD**
Bible Exposition
Author of **Make Up Your Mind and Shame Off You**
speaker and founder, **Seeing Deep Ministries**

Theresa Miller has given us more than a Bible study -- she has given us a battle plan for victorious living. With wisdom, authenticity, and a deep love for Scripture, she walks us through Psalm 63, showing how David's posture toward God can shape our own response to life's hardest battles. This study is both engaging and experiential, inviting you not only to read and reflect but to step into victory through worship, prayer, and practical action. If you've ever felt overwhelmed by defeat, this study will remind you of the power that is already yours in Christ. Prepare to be strengthened, encouraged, and transformed.

—**Jennifer Dukes Lee**
Bible study teacher
author of **Growing Slow**
and **It's All Under Control**

Introduction

How do you walk in victory when your head is spinning with defeat?

I am so glad you asked. We have heard that victory is ours because Christ defeated death on the cross. Therefore, we can claim our victory. If you are anything like me a few years ago, this is the point where you roll your eyes over cliches that do not seem to work. Or you dutifully ignore those feelings of defeat because you believe victory should work that way. You proclaim victory, and all the doubts disappear. You try harder and wonder what is wrong with you. You try again and eventually give up on a dream you thought God called you to. You justify your reasons with ideas like, "I'm not ready," "I'm not cut out for this," or "This is just who I am." You stop believing in the power of the cross and Christ's victory over death (over defeated feelings). You assume it applies to Christians, but not to you personally. What are we missing?

Walking in victory has become a familiar concept we quickly say "Amen!" to, but do not fully understand how to apply. We understand the who, what, and why, but become stumped on the how. The how is not try, try, and try again. It's not even about the why. It's about Who. Now that you have this study in your hands, we will explore together how, by better understanding *who* God is. Allow me first to lay a foundation.

Background

It is one thing to *proclaim* victory and another to *walk* in that victory confidently.

This conundrum recently hit me as I stood in the kitchen agreeing with my sister about Jesus' victory. It's a comforting truth, yet a statement I hear we Christians toss around like a magic antidote to feelings of doubt and fear. Within a couple of days of that conversation, I felt bruised and broken, my head spinning with feelings of defeat like a tornado thrashing a strong shelter.

At that moment, if I had heard one more Christian exclaim, "We have victory in Jesus," I was going to explode! As I honestly and vulnerably wrestled with how to apply Christ's victory to my everyday battles, the Lord brought me to Psalm 63. Yes, that is the chapter we all know for the popular verse about God's steadfast love being better than life (v. 3). Yet that comforting verse was not what stopped me in my tracks. The last verse did.

But the king shall rejoice in God; all who swear by him shall exult, for the mouths of liars will be stopped.

Psalm 63:11

Those last few verses jolted me into the future tense, where David prophesies the advancement of his anointing in light of the truth that the mouth of liars will not have the final say. Wow, I needed that jolt and began working backward from there to discover and emulate David's confidence.

Psalm 63 beautifully condenses David's many postures before the Lord, which we see throughout the Psalms. The wilderness setting of Psalm 63 helps us make the powerful connection between David's posture before the Lord, his continuous victories, and our ultimate victory. Although not perfect, David points us to Christ, the Anointed One.

The key concept is that David did not just turn up the praise music and proclaim victory, and that was that. If that were the case, there would have been no need for the preceding ten verses, or any other Psalm penned by David. He battled lies, rejection, betrayal, depression, and deep grief. Yet David leaned into his victory through six stunning spiritual postures described in Psalm 63. Through these continual postures, David is shown victory repeatedly. By the end of Psalm 63, he confidently proclaims that victory will have the final say, along with the advancement of his anointing as king long before he reigns as king of Israel.

How Anointing Impacts Our Victory

Psalm 20:6 says, "Now this I know: The Lord gives victory to his anointed. He answers him from his heavenly sanctuary with the victorious power of his right hand." (NIV) To sum up, anointed describes a person who is chosen for God's purposes. The Lord gives us victory because He seals us by the Holy Spirit as children of God, receiving all that is His. He gives us the power to discern and accomplish the divine work He has intended for us to do (Eph. 1:13). Furthermore, He protects us from the enemy. When we fully trust God in our anointing amidst our difficult circumstances and relationships, without shrinking back, it is a surefire way we can attest to His victory in our lives.

However, it is not automatic. It is a partnership with Christ we choose to humbly lean into and arm ourselves for the inevitable spiritual battle ahead.

Armed for Victory

The enemy is on a mission to keep us from living in our anointing because he knows God gives victory to His anointed. Although we are not defeated in Christ, the enemy only needs to make us feel we are. Feelings of defeat prevent us from forging ahead and cause us to shrink back. This is exactly what the enemy wants. He will do anything to keep us from receiving all God has for us.

Ephesians 6:12–13 professes the profound truth that our battle is not with flesh and blood and prescribes how to stand against the enemy by taking up the whole armor of God.

What does taking up the whole armor of God look like? I am convinced David displayed this in the wilderness of Judah by comforting himself in the Lord. Because God's presence consumed David, His grace equipped David with truth, righteousness, readiness, faith, and the sword of the Spirit. David fully armed himself when he acknowledged and sought God, meditated on His truths, overflowed with praise, and chose to remain near. Furthermore, David's protection and ultimate victory foreshadowed Christ, the Anointed One, our Salvation (Victory), through the gospel of peace.

In the same way, we arm ourselves for victory by fully leaning into God's presence, our source of power and strength.

Getting Back to Work

Do feelings of defeat threaten you when you pursue areas God has called you to? Those pursuits usher us into wide open spaces of vulnerability, much like the wilderness David faced. It does not matter how long we've been Christians or how deep our faith is. The enemy works overtime with his tactics, particularly when threatened that we will get a job done.

Victory is not avoiding the enemy's schemes (discomfort, fear, or intimidation). It is not getting the enemy to back off by backing down (settling into our comforts). Victory is holding our weapon with one hand (readiness) and getting back to work with the other (stepping into our calling), receiving all God has for us, and fulfilling all He has called us to (see Nehemiah 4:17). The tension in Psalm 63 of David's experience offers a breathtaking example of this.

Does proclaiming victory fall flat, discouragement set in, and conquering it seem impossible? Whether you feel paralyzed by fear, wounded by people, or abandoned by God, this study is for you.

What to Expect

Expect to deepen your trust relationship with Jesus.
Expect to take risks.
Expect to be blown away by God.

As you trust God in taking the steps of faith He is calling you to, you will be blown away by His faithfulness throughout your progress. If you are a woman who understands your bankruptcy without an active presence of God in your life and has an earnest desire for Him, then sit tight. Together we are going to accomplish amazing things in God's strength.

Over the next six weeks, we will peer into Psalm 63 primarily from the English Standard Version, observing key attributes of David that show how walking in victory is not automatic simply because we are Christians. It's a deliberate posture before the Lord. Each consecutive week we'll see how David:

1. Humbly acknowledges God as *his* God.
2. Earnestly seeks God's presence.
3. Remembers God's power and glory while meditating on His truth.
4. Praises God no matter his circumstance.
5. Cleaves to God as though his strength depends on it.
6. Confidently proclaims victory in the advancement of his anointing.

What You Will Need
> The study workbook
> Your Bible
> A journal
> Pen (and highlighters if you like to highlight)
> Sketch pencils or colored pencils (optional)
> Spotify or YouTube (Spotify Playlist QR Code provided in Appendix Three)

How This Study Works
We will practice David's various postures in Psalm 63, as we reflect on the truth of God's Word and how it applies to our lives. The beginning of each day offers the opportunity to check your posture. I suggest reading the Introduction, ending with the prayer, and following the meditative passage of Psalm 63 before Day One. Day One presents a devotional for each week's theme. Days Two and Four offer commentary-style devotions, digging deeper into the theme and prompting you to discover truths in Scripture. Day Three focuses on a song to soak in, Scripture to reflect on, and a prompt to scribble your thoughts, through reflective writing or artistic creation. Day Five wraps up the week with concluding thoughts to consider and practical application for your weekend. At the end of each week, you will also be blessed by prayerful Scripture-informed revelation.

These practices have become a powerful vehicle for communing with God and a means for healing and clarity in my life. I pray that the reflections, discoveries, and practices throughout this study will also be a powerful means of communion and healing for you. Finally, we will discover how Week One intricately ties into each of the following weeks and makes Week Six possible. Are you ready to experience victory in the areas you feel most defeated? I cannot wait to go on this journey with you!

A Note about Context

David fled from his enemies twice in Scripture: once from King Saul and once from his son, Absalom. Scholars are divided on which occasion David is reflecting upon in Psalm 63. For this Bible study, we will focus on David's flight from Saul. While we cannot be certain which event Psalm 63 references, it does not diminish the truth of the Psalm. My hope and desire for you is to emulate David's profound devotion to God, regardless of the circumstances.

Check Your Posture

James 4:6 reminds us that God gives grace to the humble. This is not because humility earns us grace but puts us in the position to receive it. How do we do this? James 4 goes on to prescribe that we must submit to God. This means we surrender to Him as our Supreme Ruler and King, receiving the benefits of His reign. This is the only way to resist the devil. Therefore, before each day, we will "check our posture" by praying Psalm 139:23–24:

> *Search me, O God, and know my heart! Try me and know my thoughts! And see if there be any grievous way in me, and lead me in the way everlasting!*
>
> Psalm 139:23–24

Definitions
(According to Websters Dictionary 1828)

Victory:
Victory in the spiritual sense is "the advantage or superiority gained over spiritual enemies, over passions and appetites, or over temptations, or in any struggle or competition."
> *Thanks be to God, which giveth us the victory, through our Lord Jesus Christ.*
>   1 Corinthians 15:57 (KJV).

Posture:
"Disposition; frame; as the posture of the soul."

Defeat:
"Overthrow; loss of battle; the check, rout, or destruction of an army by the victory of an enemy."
Christ defeated death, yet the enemy is on a mission to make us feel defeated by feeling beaten down, discouraged, and fearful. Defeat is not our reality unless we allow it to be.

Wilderness:
"A desert; a tract of land or region uncultivated and uninhabited by human beings, whether a forest or a wide barren plain. In the United States, it is applied only to a forest. In Scripture, it is applied frequently to the deserts of Arabia. The Israelites wandered in the wilderness forty years."
Although David was in a literal wilderness, we will define wilderness in the spiritual sense. The dry and weary land of our hearts, where we earnestly desire God's presence.

Opposition:
"Resistance; as the opposition of enemies. Virtue will break through all opposition."
Although David's opposition was a physical army pursuing him, we will refer to opposition in the spiritual sense. The enemy's lies and the battle for our mind Christians are up against.

Enemy:

"In theology, and by way of eminence, the enemy is the Devil; the archfiend."

Lie:
"To utter falsehood with an intention to deceive, or with an immoral design."

A lie in the spiritual sense is simply anything we believe about ourselves that is contrary to what God has established as truth.

Anoint:
"To prepare, in allusion to the consecrating use of oil.
"To anoint the head with oil, Psalm 23 seems to signify to communicate the consolations of the Holy Spirit.
"The use of oil in consecrations was of high antiquity. Kings, prophets and priests were set apart or consecrated to their offices by the use of oil. Hence the peculiar application of the term anointed to Jesus Christ."

For us, anoint means to be set apart for God's services. When we read about anointing in the New Testament, it refers to all believers. God anoints believers today through the power of the Holy Spirit to accomplish specific tasks and bless others.

Humility:
"In theology, humility consists in lowliness of mind; a deep sense of one's own unworthiness in the sight of God, self-abasement, penitence for sin, and submission to the divine will."
But humility comes before honor.

Proverbs 18:12

Serving the Lord with all humility of mind.

Acts 20:19

Mindful:
"Attentive; regarding with care; bearing in mind; heedful; observant."
What is man that you are mindful of him, and the son of man that you care for him?

Psalm 8:4

This term is compatible with Christianity when rooted in the Word of God and connecting with Him. Think of it as our minds existing with God. It is having the mind of Christ (1 Cor. 2:14–16) by connecting with God through His Word and in His presence. For this study, we will refer to it as "a posture of presence."

Psalm 63

Optional: Listen to the sixteen-minute meditative reading of Psalm 63 by EKKO Church on the playlist.

A Psalm of David, when he was in the wilderness of Judah.

> O God, you are my God; earnestly I seek you;
> my soul thirsts for you;
> my flesh faints for you,
> as in a dry and weary land where there is no water.
>
> So I have looked upon you in the sanctuary,
> beholding your power and glory.
>
> Because your steadfast love is better than life,
> my lips will praise you.
>
> So I will bless you as long as I live;
> in your name I will lift up my hands.
>
> My soul will be satisfied as with fat and rich food,
> and my mouth will praise you with joyful lips,
>
> when I remember you upon my bed,
> and meditate on you in the watches of the night;
>
> for you have been my help,
> and in the shadow of your wings I will sing for joy.
>
> My soul clings to you;
> your right hand upholds me.
>
> But those who seek to destroy my life
> shall go down into the depths of the earth;
>
> they shall be given over to the power of the sword;
> they shall be a portion for jackals.
>
> But the king shall rejoice in God;
> all who swear by him shall exult,

for the mouths of liars will be stopped.

Heavenly Father, *You are victorious. You are compassionate and patient. You care about the details of my life whether I am wandering through a wilderness or thriving on a mountaintop. You use everything for my good and Your glory. I confess I feel discouraged in my wilderness moments. I have not trusted Your plans for me. I have not trusted the full essence of my salvation. But you are a merciful God who uses my wilderness moments to prepare me more fully for Your anointing on my life. Help me to open my heart to Your presence over the next six weeks. Reveal the power of Your presence, promises, and of prayer. Finally, reveal the power of Your anointing on my life so that I may arm myself for victory every single time. In Jesus' name, amen.*

Week One

A Posture of Humility

"The life of true holiness is rooted in the soil of awed adoration."
Rediscovering Holiness: Know the Fullness of Life with God, J.I Packer[1]

---

[1] Packer, J.I., *Rediscovering Holiness: Know the Fullness of Life with God*, Baker Books, Grand Rapids, Michigan, 2009, pp. 73.

Day One
Humbly Acknowledge God

Check Your Posture: Open your hands and heart, and pray Psalm 139:23–24:

> *Search me, O God, and know my heart! Try me and know my thoughts! And see if there be any grievous way in me, and lead me in the way everlasting!*

Devotional: True Confidence

> *O God, you are my God; my soul thirsts for you; my flesh faints for you, as in a dry and weary land where there is no water.*
>
> Psalm 63:1

True confidence begins with humility. That is, allowing God to be all.

A few winters ago, I felt a lull in my faith walk. My prayers felt shallow, and doubt overwhelmed my everyday circumstances. As I sought the Lord, He prompted me to start my mornings face down before Him, proclaiming who He is. I admit it felt awkward, unnatural, and uncomfortable at first. Yet it changed me. That practice alone was a position of humility that boldly gave God the glory He was due. It changed how I prayed, deepened my thanksgiving, and elevated my belief.

Hebrews 4:16 (KJV) offers a profound statement for approaching God: *Let us therefore come boldly unto the throne of grace, that we may obtain mercy and find grace to help in time of need.* This charge echoes David's confidence in his relationship with God in the wilderness of Judah throughout 1 Samuel and as demonstrated in Psalm 63, where David acknowledges who God is in a relevant and personal way.

Once David, the young, confident shepherd boy, is anointed to be the next king of Israel, he displays unsurpassed courage and trust. Knowing the God of Israel is with him, he selects some stones and a sling and nails Goliath, the Philistine, between the eyes. When David presents the head of Goliath to King Saul, Saul takes him in as his own and places him at the head of his army. David's fame grows exponentially, and Saul soon becomes jealous. Saul and his army drive David and a small army into the wilderness of Judah, where he flees for his life for more than ten years. Grief-stricken, it is here we are shown David acknowledging his deep allegiance to God with a simple address: *Oh God, you are my God...*

Why does this matter? This one phrase communicates more than what meets the eye. David names God twice in the same breath, offering two different meanings. Here David acknowledges that God, (*Elohim* – the

Supreme Ruler over the universe)[2] is *his* God (*El*—his strength).[3] David does not treat Him like any other god, keeping Him at a distance with a false sense of unworthiness. David bases his bold approach on who God is in light of his weakness. David acknowledges the supreme ruler of the universe, who transcends time and space, as his personal strength.

Have you thought about that? God is not only the God of the universe but also the one who considers you down to the subatomic makeup of your being. Psalm 139:13–14 poetically assures us of this in David's confession of praise: *For you formed my inward parts; you knitted me together in my mother's womb. I praise you, for I am fearfully and wonderfully made. Wonderful are your works; my soul knows it very well.*

God masterfully weaves your personality, gifts, and talents into your DNA. In addition, Genesis 17:8 indicates that God intended to be your personal God from the beginning through His covenant made with Abraham: *And I will give to you and to your offspring after you the land of your sojourning, all the land of Canaan, for an everlasting possession, and I will be their God.* God made the ultimate way to Himself personally through Jesus. Oh, how He loves us!

We don't have to come to God perfectly. His grace covers our imperfections. He invites us to come humbly, however, understanding that the throne of grace (Jesus) is sufficient to fulfill His promises in our lives, as believers (2 Cor. 12:9). When we acknowledge His grace and sufficiency, we can trust His purpose and promises. In that space, we can come boldly with a confident expectation for what He will do.

While we will dig into seeking God next week, will you join me today in beginning your prayer simply by proclaiming who God is in light of your weakness?

Because true confidence begins with humility.

For Further Application: Throughout this study, we will practice proclaiming who God is at the beginning of each prayer. Why do you think it is important to acknowledge who God is before making your requests known? Write your thoughts below:

---

[2] "H430 - 'ĕlōhîm - Strong's Hebrew Lexicon (kjv)." Blue Letter Bible. Web. 18 Jan, 2024. <https://www.blueletterbible.org/lexicon/h430/kjv/wlc/0-1/>.
[3] "H410 - 'ēl - Strong's Hebrew Lexicon (kjv)." Blue Letter Bible. Web. 18 Jan, 2024. <https://www.blueletterbible.org/lexicon/h410/kjv/wlc/0-1/>.

Oh God, *You are **my** God – the Creator and Supreme God over all, yet You are near. For You formed my inward parts; You knitted me together in my mother's womb. I praise You, for I am fearfully and wonderfully made (Ps. 139:13–14). You are my strength when I am weak, my defense when I am vulnerable, and my protection when I am in harm's way. Thank You for relentlessly pursuing and drawing me to You. Help me to boldly and humbly come before Your throne of grace each day to receive the mercy and grace of Your redemption that You have intended for my life. In Jesus' name, amen.*

> *The fear of the* LORD *is the beginning of wisdom, and the knowledge of the Holy One is insight.*
>
> Proverbs 9:10

Day Two
Acknowledging Who God Is
Oh God...

Check Your Posture: Open your hands and heart, and pray Psalm 139:23–24:
> *Search me, O God, and know my heart! Try me and know my thoughts!*
> *And see if there be any grievous way in me, and lead me in the way*
> *everlasting!*

Commentary, Part One:
Imagine a world where a select few know God and idols prolifically permeate the pagan land. This was true for David when he cried to God in the wilderness, *Oh God, you are my God*. His bold proclamation, especially for his time, reveals confidence and deep allegiance to the one true God. It is as though David is crying out, "Oh Supreme God and Creator of the universe—the one and only God, you are my source of strength!"

David models that proper respect and honor for God begins with adoration of Him. Although many of David's psalms start with a desperate plea, he always turns the plea to acknowledge who God is. Beginning with adoration, even before making our requests or expressing thanksgiving, can be a profound practice that changes our heart's posture. If adoration before thanksgiving is a new concept, consider how our default thanksgiving typically amounts to the good things in our lives. When we offer adoration for God's character, we are more readily reminded of His goodness, which sustains us even through the hard times.

This does not mean God will not accept our desperate pleas if ordered differently. In Psalm 16, 43, and 143, for example, David's first words are, *Preserve me, O God, Vindicate me, O God*, and *Hear my prayer, O LORD; give ear to my pleas for mercy!* He then transitions his pleas to acknowledging God by remembering His character. We see this often throughout the varied Psalms. If a plea is all your desperate heart can muster, then start there. We just can't stay there. We must allow our plea to guide us to God's everlasting character.

The point is not that we become legalistic, but that we honor and welcome the God of the universe to be *our* God—a God we can be honest with in our lament. We honor and welcome our just and holy God who fights for us and strengthens us as a reflection of our trust in Him.

In Timothy Keller's book, *Prayer*, he affirms, "Praise and adoration are the necessary preconditions for the proper formulation and motivation of all other kinds of prayer." (Keller 190)[4]

Our adoration of God sets the tone for the rest of our prayer because naming God's character is an act of remembrance and trust in who He is and what He can do. As we will see in the upcoming weeks, David prays with this reverence to God throughout his most difficult wilderness experience.

Our culture is not too far from David's. Idols permeate our thoughts and lives. God is an idea to most people and is becoming more and more offensive to our culture. Our acknowledgment of God in all His power will be our key source of strength in times of desperate need. No other source will suffice.

Questions

Read Matthew 6:9. How does Jesus teach us to begin our prayer?

Do you think the Jews were accustomed to referencing God as their Father before Jesus taught them how to pray? What significance stands out to you in the prayer's opening?

Name the attributes of God the Psalmist begins his prayer within each of the following Psalms.

Psalm 8:

Psalm 18:

Psalm 104:

Psalm 144:

---

[4] Keller, Timothy. *Prayer: Experiencing Awe and Intimacy with God.* Dutton/Penguin Group, New York, New York, 2014.

Read Psalm 102. How do the first eleven verses contrast with the following sixteen?

What word indicates this change in direction (v.12)?

What is the difference in verb tense?

What quality does the change of verb tense indicate in the Psalmist?

Read 1 Samuel 13:8–14 (also see Chapter 15: 22–24). What reason do verses 13 and 14 offer for God removing the kingdom of Israel from Saul?

When the prophet Samuel announced that God had taken the kingdom from Saul and given it to a man after His own heart, what was God ultimately looking for in a king?

What does David's bold acknowledgment of God in Psalm 63:1 reflect about him?

How did Saul, anointed by God to serve as the first king of Israel, fail to uphold this humble characteristic (v. 8-12)?

What does it mean to you to be a person after God's own heart (what do you think God desires from you)?

What does it mean to address God with reverence and adoration in a culture that is rapidly canceling the idea of a Supreme God?

Oh God, you are Elohim, the Supreme God and Creator of the universe. You are all-knowing, always present, and all-powerful. I praise You because You are worthy to be praised. You have been my rock, my fortress, and my Savior. How good You are to me. Help me to be a woman after Your own heart as I learn to trust You even more and walk in obedience to Your call and Word. Help me continually proclaim allegiance to You, the one true God, and fully depend on Your strength. In Jesus' name, amen.

O LORD, our Lord, how majestic is your name in all the earth! You have set your glory above the heavens.

Psalm 8:1

Day Three
Our Confession

Check Your Posture: Open your hands and heart and pray Psalm 139:23–24:

> *Search me, O God, and know my heart! Try me and know my thoughts! And see if there be any grievous way in me, and lead me in the way everlasting!*

Soak, Scripture, and Scribble

Soak: Search and listen to the song, "I Am," by Jill Phillips, while resting in God's presence.

Going deeper: if you are physically able, try soaking in God's presence with your face to the ground, as you listen.

(Soak)

Scripture focus: Psalm 23, 1 Samuel 16:11, Psalm 51:1–18, Hebrews 13:20–21, Hebrews 4:14–16

God is holy. Yet He will tenderly comfort you like a mother while you rest. Can you sense how great, yet how near God is to you?

It's easy to shout God's praises when we're on top of the world and feel nothing can threaten our peace and joy in Christ. It's not as easy in the valley where we feel weary, vulnerable, and lonely. A pastoral friend once explained the mountaintop as the place where we rest. The valley is where our faith is tested. Most of our days will be spent in the tension of allowing God to work out our faith in the valley by learning to surrender, trust, and obey Him.

When we believe and acknowledge these truths about who God is, when we believe in our hearts and confess with our mouths who Christ is, we will have the capacity in Christ to live out our confession of faith even through our wilderness wanderings.

Throughout the Psalms, David confesses his faith each time he acknowledges who God is in light of his weaknesses and despite the wilderness he is in. We must too.

Questions

Read Psalm 23. How does David describe who God is to him in this passage?

21

How might David's acknowledgment of God as his shepherd reflect his understanding of God (see 1 Sam. 16:11)?

David's Psalm mirrors his soul. Where does David imply his soul is?

David's wilderness experience contrasts who God is amidst his wilderness, like sheep led by their shepherd to streams of water. What attribute of God stands out to you in Psalm 23? Why?

Read Hebrew 4:14–16. For what reason does the author implore us to hold fast (seize or retain) our confession (v.14)?

There were times in David's life, later as king, that he did not hold fast to his confession and seek God through temptation. Sin hardens hearts. It was not until the prophet Nathan called David out on his sin and only after he lost a son due to sin that he was humbled (softened) to repent once again.

Read Psalm 51. On what does David base his bold confession of sin and need for God (v. 1)?

What does God delight in when we come before Him with our sins (v.17)?

For David and us, our confession of sin is just as important as our confession of faith.

Scribble: Begin your confession by acknowledging who God is in your life. Consider where you are with God. Be honest. Do not hold back. Tell Him your thoughts, concerns, worries, and fears. What questions do you have? What does God's holiness and redemption mean to you? Conclude by confessing what areas you can turn from to draw closer to God.

Optional: Include an illustration expressing your confession of faith.

> *Oh God, I boldly come before Your throne of grace acknowledging my need for You. You are holy. You are constant. You are wise. Thank You that You are always near me. Thank You for Your unfailing love and presence that brings me comfort and rest. May Your Spirit guide me in all my ways and lead me in the way everlasting. In Jesus' name, amen.*

> *This was according to the eternal purpose that he has realized in Christ Jesus our Lord, in whom we have boldness and access with confidence through our faith in him.*
>
> Ephesians 3:11–12

Day Four
Acknowledging Who God Is
My God

Check Your Posture: Open your hands and heart, and pray Psalm 139:23–24:

> *Search me, O God, and know my heart! Try me and know my thoughts! And see if there be any grievous way in me, and lead me in the way everlasting!*

Commentary, Part Two:

David agonizes over the absence of God's presence in the wilderness. He boldly proclaims allegiance to the one true God and acknowledges Him intimately: *Oh God, you are my God* (Ps. 63:1a). This intimate address displays David's deep connection and complete confidence in God. It is like him saying, "I've seen you do it before. You can do it again!" El is the Hebrew word used for God in this context, meaning strength. It is the same Hebrew meaning of the phrase used by Jesus on the cross when He cries out to the Father, *My God, My God, why have you forsaken me?* (Mt. 27:46). This fulfills the prophecy of David's words in Psalm 22:1.

As horrendous as Jesus' physical suffering was, the true agony He experienced on the cross was God's wrath and His loss of fellowship with Him. This is the cup He asked God to take from Him in the Garden of Gethsemane, according to His will. According to David Guzik, "Repeatedly in the Old Testament, a cup is a powerful picture of the wrath and judgment of God."[5] Rather than taking the cup from Jesus and eliminating the agony He was experiencing, God sent angels to strengthen Him.

Driven into the wilderness, David is far from God's presence, found in the Ark of the Covenant in the Holy of Holies of the Tabernacle. He feels agony in this absence of God's presence. Yet despite his deep longing for God, God does not remove David's suffering or the enemy driving him. Instead, God strengthens David in his desperate plea for God Himself.

Think about when you have felt distant from God's presence. Recall the dry, impoverished, and miserable feeling of isolation. Our wilderness and even David's cannot compare to Jesus' agony, yet Jesus can sympathize with us. Jesus, too, was led to the wilderness where He became depleted and weary, only to be tempted by the devil. God allows

---

[5] Guzik, David. *Matthew 26 - Jesus' Betrayal and Arrest*. Enduring Word, 1996-2024, enduringword.com

our wildernesses to meet, strengthen, and transform us.

Sadly, the world offers empty and immediate remedies of comfort outside of God. Yet, Thomas a` Kempis in *The Imitation of Christ* reminds us that in our spiritual progress, "the spiritual life does not consist only in having the grace of comfort." He expounds that when comfort has been withdrawn, we ought to endure it with humility, self-denial, and patience — continuing in prayer and attention to our spiritual life. (Kempis 123)[6]

David does not doubt his lack outside of God's presence. He is desperate to experience God in the wilderness where he is exposed daily to the elements — thirsty, exhausted, and weary. Yet putting his confidence in God also means he trusts Him, as Jesus displayed on the cross.

The wilderness is a metaphor for our dry and depleted souls, desiring living water through God's presence. For whatever reason we find ourselves passing through a spiritual wilderness, we too must understand our desperate need for God.

Questions

Read Psalm 22:1–10. This is one of many Psalms that give context to David's cry to *his* God in the wilderness. For what reason does David trust God as *his* God (v. 4–5, 9–10)?

How does David's experience in the wilderness foreshadow what Jesus went through leading up to the cross (v. 6-8 and Mt. 27:43)?

Read Luke 22: 39–46. Does it surprise you that Jesus' agony over a loss of fellowship with God upon the cross would be greater than the physical mutilation and mockery He endured? In addition, in His most difficult moments, Jesus desperately desired the support of His disciples. What does this say about the importance of godly fellowship and support in your relationship with God? What does it say about your obedience to His call on your life?

---

[6] Kempis, Thomas a`. *The Imitation of Christ*. Bridge-Logos Publishers, North Brunswick, NJ, 1999.

What does 2 Corinthians 5:21 say God's purpose was for breaking fellowship with Jesus on the cross?

How does Isaiah 53:4–6 communicate God's love for you?

God desires a deep relationship with you. Pause and consider how God has pursued your heart and an intimate relationship with you.

> *Oh God, you are my God! You are El, my strength. Although You may not choose to remove my wilderness or suffering, You are a God who is near, who strengthens me, and carries me when I am depleted. Thank You for Your measureless love and the incredible suffering Jesus bore on the cross so that I may be free from my shackles and brought back into fellowship with You. Thank You that You are a God who sympathizes with my struggles and infuses Your power and strength into my weakness as I turn to and trust in You. Help me to trust You more fully and may Your presence always be upon me – before, beside, and behind me. In Jesus' name, amen.*

> *I have been crucified with Christ. It is no longer I who live, but Christ who lives in me. And the life I now live in the flesh I live by faith in the Son of God, who loved me and gave himself for me.*
> Galatians 2:20

Day Five
God's Presence in the Wilderness

Check Your Posture: Open your hands and heart, and pray Psalm 139:23–
24:

> *Search me, O God, and know my heart! Try me and know my
> thoughts! And see if there be any grievous way in me, and lead me in
> the way everlasting!*

Ponder and Personalized Practice

> *Be still, and know that I am God. I will be exalted among the nations, I
> will be exalted in the earth!*
>
> Psalm 46:10

This week we explored adoring and worshiping God as our Supreme
God yet receiving Him as our personal God. He is the King of Kings and
Lord of Lords! When we find ourselves in a wilderness period, God is
calling us to be still and know that He is God. The gift of the wilderness
strips us of all that we can do for Him and calls us into His presence.

As we close this week, I invite you to ponder and practice the lessons
you have gleaned, beginning with acknowledging who God is to you.

Ponder: Personalize five attributes that describe who God has been
to you personally in your life or that have stood out to you this week (e.g.,
my strength):

1. My _____
2. My _____
3. My _____
4. My _____
5. My _____

Practice: If the weather permits, find a spot in nature and sit in
silence. This can be as simple as a local park or your backyard. If the
weather does not permit, sit near a window and peer out. Consider these
attributes of God. Can you feel a sense of peace wash over you as you
consider who God is to you today? Write about what God may be
speaking to your heart in this space.

Father God, *You are my (name the attributes you recorded here). I* confess I have kept You at a distance. You gently pursue me, never scold me, or condemn me, and bring life and restoration to my soul. Thank You for intricately creating me and carrying out Your plan to be in a relationship with me, through Christ. Thank You for the grace to come boldly before Your throne in an intimate, personal way, and for giving me the wholeness of Yourself. Help me to run toward You even when you feel distant and to trust You with the broken pieces I offer. In Jesus' name, amen.

> Oh come, let us worship and bow down; let us kneel before the LORD, our Maker!
>
> Psalm 95:6

Scripture Informed Revelation

Beloved,

You are beautiful because you are Mine.

Dear one, there are several ways to abide in Me, but one necessary posture, as one who belongs to Me—humility.

Your humble heart knows that I am God, and you are not. Your surrendered heart knows that I am *your* God. Do you feel My strength empowering your weakness?

You will trust Me to hold your broken pieces together for a greater purpose in your humbled posture.

I am *your* God. I knit you together in your mother's womb. I am not surprised by the world I have intricately designed you for and placed you in. I am not alarmed by your generation's fallen state; nor am I baffled by your fallen heritage. I am not surprised by your fallen circumstances. I do not take away the circumstances that come with a fallen world but walk with you through them. I will never leave you or forsake you.

When you weep, I will weep. When you fall, I will pick you up. When you wander, I will wait. When you return, I will rejoice. You have *everything* in Me. You are safe with Me. Make your home in Me. You are Mine.

Psalm 51:17
Isaiah 41:10
Isaiah 43:1
2 Corinthians 12:9
Psalm 41:12
Matthew 6:34
Psalm 139:13
Psalm 16:8
Deuteronomy 31:6
Psalm 34:18
Psalm 145:14
Luke 15:20
Psalm 27:5
Psalm 91:9

Week Two

A Posture of Prayer

"Why do we seem so hesitant to receive this filling of God's Spirit? I would suggest it's not because we are so scared of being possessed by God; rather, it is because we are so determined to find the water on our own. Believe me, we can't find it. We can only let it find us by stopping the relentless search long enough to turn our thirst into prayer – and then to wait for the Spirit."

Sacred Thirst, M. Craig Barnes[7]

---

[7] Barnes, M. Craig, *Sacred Thirst*. Zondervan, Grand Rapids, Michigan, 2001, pp.115.

Day One
Earnestly Seek God's Presence

Check Your Posture: Open your hands and heart, and pray Psalm 139:23–24:

> *Search me, O God, and know my heart! Try me and know my thoughts! And see if there be any grievous way in me, and lead me in the way everlasting!*

Devotional
When Fear and Doubt Lurk

> *Earnestly I seek you; my soul thirsts for you; my flesh faints for you, as in a dry and weary land where there is no water.*
>
> Psalm 63:1b

Fear and doubt lurk at every corner.

The doubts kept coming as I beat myself up over a minor inconvenience. I had gone on a walk with my husband and came home late to a Zoom meeting that had started without me. The problem was that I was supposed to initiate the meeting and ran head-on into the enemy's mental attacks.

"How could you drop the ball?"

"You're not good enough."

"You have nothing to contribute."

"They don't even need you."

These messages may not have been a reality, but they sped through my mind so fast it made me dizzy. Was this when I was supposed to proclaim victory? At that moment, I was more desperate to escape defeat than to overcome it.

Defeating statements like these proclaim doom over our lives. Yet if we're proclaiming doom, we're certainly in no position to claim victory.

David reveals a different picture when he cries out to God over King Saul's unjust pursuit of his life in his continuation of Psalm 63:1: *Oh God, you are my God, earnestly I seek you; my soul thirsts for you; my flesh faints for you, as in a dry and weary land where there is no water."*

When Saul drives David to the wilderness of Judah, David leaves behind the comfort of friendship, loyalty, anointing, and familiarity. David could no longer adore God and worship Him in the sanctuary, as he had richly experienced in the past. Removing God's presence and favor will be the true test of our desire for God. In times of trouble, will we despise God or desire Him more?

In this passage, David does not fearfully flee and hide from his enemies in the wilderness of Judah, alone and bewildered. We don't hear him questioning God or God's anointing over him. David eagerly pursues God through the wilderness with urgency and an insatiable thirst for His presence. He compares his deep desire for God to a desert where he can find no water.

Charles Spurgeon amplifies this thirst in the following way:

"Thirst is an insatiable longing after that which is one of the most essential supports of life; there is no reasoning with it, no forgetting it, no despising it, no overcoming it by stoic indifference. Thirst will be heard; the whole man must yield to its power." (Spurgeon 1879)[8]

Because of his insatiable thirst, David finds God in the middle of his desperate and chaotic circumstances. The wilderness did not eliminate God's presence or David's anointing. It prepared him for it by trusting God more fully. In our spiritual battles, evil may appear to win for a time but never has the final say. Even in our struggle, Genesis 50:20 and Romans 8:28 remind us that God will use every one of our circumstances for good, as we seek and trust Him more than anything else.

As for you, you meant evil against me, but God meant it for good, to bring it about that many people should be kept alive, as they are today.

Genesis 50:20

And we know that for those who love God all things work together for good,[a] for those who are called according to his purpose.

Romans 8:28

We don't have to despise our feelings of lack. It is okay to bring our complaints and laments to God as David did. Admitting our vulnerabilities before Him is necessary because we will never truly claim our victory until we first acknowledge our brokenness. This is where God meets us, right here in the middle of our mess, our valley, and our thirsty desert. This is where we too will most thirst for God's presence. We can trust that God will quench our thirst in our isolation and those dark, long watchful hours of the night.

Fear and doubt may lurk in our pursuits; but cannot prevail in God's presence.

Today I challenge you to pause and acknowledge any doubt spinning through your mind as you earnestly seek God.

---

[8] Spurgeon, Charles. *The Treasury of David: The Complete Seven Volumes.* Vol. 3, E-book Ed., 2012.

For Further Application: Confess your need for God, as an extension of your confession from Week One.

Father, You are my all in all. I do not have to measure up or gain another person's approval to be accepted and loved by You. I confess that I feel inadequate when I let someone else or myself down. But You are gracious. Thank You for extending Your grace through Your Son, Jesus. Please help me to fully receive Your grace so I may extend it to others. I trust that You hear my every plea and that I am enough in You. In Jesus' name, amen.

Now to him who is able to do far more abundantly than all that we ask or think, according to the power at work within us.

Ephesians 3:20

Day Two
Understanding Our Need for God
Thirst

Check Your Posture: Open your hands and heart, and pray Psalm 139:23–24:

> *Search me, O God, and know my heart! Try me and know my thoughts! And see if there be any grievous way in me, and lead me in the way everlasting!*

Commentary, Part One:

Imagine being in a desert or on a long excursion without water. How desperate would you feel? I've been there. Running thirteen miles down the Big Horn Mountains with my sister to the small town of Buffalo, WY, I underestimated the amount of water I should bring along. Before we were halfway to our destination, my sister and I were rationing small sips from her bottle. Once we reached the foothills, we ran alongside a bacteria-filled river. The enticing water source proved inaccessible without a filter. We were running on empty with several miles still to our destination. I was desperate for water.

Thirsting for God parallels our thirst for water because Scripture identifies God with water throughout. John 4:10 says that Jesus is the living water and John 7:38–39 refers to the Holy Spirit as streams of living water.

This thirst is like the desperation David sought God with—a desperate desire needing an immediate response. Indifference was not an option. There was no denying his insatiable thirst.

But to thirst for God means first recognizing our need for Him. We may thirst deeply, yet foolishly drink from contaminated sources that bring scarcity and fatality to our bodies. We must know the Source and where to find it so our thirst can be fully quenched, and our souls revived. "Blessed are those who hunger and thirst for righteousness, for they shall be satisfied" (Mt. 5:6).

This is how we understand our identity. We are parched souls without God. He is everything. We need Him. We need Him to walk in our anointing and fulfill our purpose in life. We can be all He created us to be when we fully trust Him.

The Spirit of God rested on David, giving him the power to walk in his anointing as future king, as he earnestly sought God to quench his thirst. That same Spirit of God raised Jesus from the dead. We are given that very same Spirit when we put our trust in Him.

This is why we must find our identity in the power of Christ's resurrected life, and nothing else. This is why we must thirst for God as though our life depends on it.

Do you thirst for God? Do you want to? Pause and tell Him about it.

Questions

Read John 4:7–15. What does Jesus tell the Samaritan woman at the well she would receive if she knew who was asking her for water?

What four things do you think Jesus caused the woman to consider with the phrase, "If you knew"? What is He implying with this phrase (v. 10)?

What does Jesus say about the water He gives in v. 14?

What sources have you sought to quench your thirst? Did it satisfy you or leave you feeling empty? Explain.

Read John 7:37–39. Who can quench our thirst?

Who may come and have their thirst quenched?

Describe the living water that Jesus references in v. 38–39?

Based on what you just read, is the water Jesus gives meant to be a one-time gulp?

How does Jesus satisfy us forever on this side of heaven?

Father, You are holy, ever-present, and all-knowing. I am desperate for You. I am desperate to know You more. Thank You for Your power in my life. Thank You that with You there is always more. Help me to trust You enough to share my heart honestly and vulnerably. Cause me to thirst for You as I pour my heart out and allow Your Spirit to quench my thirst. In Jesus' name, amen.

> For in the wilderness shall waters break out, and streams in the desert. And the parched ground shall become a pool, and the thirsty land springs of water.
>
> Isaiah 35:6-7 KJV

Day Three
Seek

Check Your Posture: Open your hands and heart, and pray Psalm 139:23–24:

> *Search me, O God, and know my heart! Try me and know my thoughts! And see if there be any grievous way in me, and lead me in the way everlasting!*

Soak, Scripture, and Scribble

Soak: Search and listen to the song, "I Surrender," by Hillsong, while resting in God's presence.

Going deeper: Consider how the Holy Spirit may be prompting your posture in His presence, as you listen.

(Soak)

Scripture Focus: Matthew 6:25-34, Ephesians 2:10

How desperate for God are you? Like the Samaritan woman at the well in yesterday's Scripture verses, I am desperate for the Lord and to know Him more. How about you?

Our thirst for God will be satisfied far more abundantly than any desire we will ever know. Desiring things in this world leaves us void within minutes because God is the only one who can completely satisfy our deepest desires and quench our insatiable thirst. He is who we are longing for. It is only God who is always enough yet offers more. The more of God we have the more of God we crave. He won't leave us empty. There is always more with God.

Do you desire God with an unquenchable thirst? God creates the thirst in reborn souls, those who believe in their hearts and confess with their mouths that Jesus is Lord over their lives. Only He can satisfy us. If we only knew He was all we needed, we would stop searching for meager sources to quench our thirst and drink from Him alone.

Have you prayed for this? If not, take a moment to commit (or recommit) your heart to Christ right now (see appendix for a first-time Commitment Prayer or a Recommitment Prayer of Complete Surrender).[9]

Questions

---

[9] See Appendix One

Read Matthew 6:25–34. Why do we need not worry about life's circumstances (Also see Matthew 7:7–11)?

For what reason does Matthew 6:33 command us to seek God first above all that we need or want?

How does seeking God and His righteousness first affect our spiritual posture?

Read Ephesians 2:10. How are our spiritual and creative gifts and works connected to seeking the Kingdom of God first in all things?

In our first-world country, is it possible we do not seek God or thirst for His presence nearly enough? Why do you think that is?

What does seeking *first* the Kingdom of God mean to you and your circumstances?

Physically speaking, David needed countless things in the wilderness. He needed shelter from climate change, food, water, protection, and a community of people who supported him. Yet David sought God's presence first. He was desperate for Him. God provided everything else David needed to sustain him.

Scribble: In what areas do you feel restless in your life? Confess any area of brokenness, lack, or grievances you need to surrender, as you earnestly seek God in prayer. Is there somebody who disappointed you that you had trusted? Do you feel angry with God? Write about this or express it artistically as an extension of your confession.

Father, You are my life source. I thank You for offering the living water that restores my soul. Quench my thirst as I seek You before all other things. In Jesus' name, amen.

But seek first the kingdom of God and his righteousness, and all these things will be added to you.

Matthew 6:33

Day Four
Understanding Our Need for God
Longing

Check Your Posture: Open your hands and heart, and pray Psalm 139:23–24:

> *Search me, O God, and know my heart! Try me and know my thoughts! And see if there be any grievous way in me, and lead me in the way everlasting!*

Commentary, Part Two:

About the end of February, I'm ready for spring. I realize January and February are Wyoming's most brutal winter months and I do not expect anything less. I simply hunker down and roll with it.

But when March first arrives, I long for spring. My soul grows a little weary gazing out to the same crunchy snow that was present the day before.

March promises spring, and although our seasons do not always cooperate with the months, a weary hope stirs. It's an achy kind of hope. We know spring is coming. We have experienced the sun melting the snow and warming our faces. We have witnessed the wet earth shooting forth new blooms, and trees budding. We yearn for spring in the dead of winter.

This is like the longing David feels in the wilderness of Judah. He experienced God's presence in the sanctuary, witnessed God's power and glory, and now longs for God in the wilderness, figuratively and literally.

C.H. Spurgeon adds, "When the wilderness caused David weariness, discomfort, and thirst, his soul cried out in unison with the desire of his flesh" (Spurgeon 1879)[10]. God meets David in his desperation—amidst the wilderness—right smack in the middle of unchanged circumstances. Amidst unchanged circumstances, joy springs forth within David.

Our longing is not meant to stir despair or restlessness. It is not something to numb, avoid, or escape. It cannot be ignored.

Our longing is meant to stir the ache of desire for God's presence, promises, and peace. It is an ache only the God of all hope can fill.

Questions

Read Psalm 13. This Psalm is one of David's Psalms of Lament. According

---

[10] Spurgeon, Charles. *The Treasury of David: The Complete Seven Volumes. Vol. 3*, E-book Ed., 2012

to *Webster's Dictionary 1828*, lament means "to mourn; to grieve; to weep or wail; to express sorrow."

What four things does David lament in v.1–2?

David felt despair. He felt God had forgotten him. Did God forget Him? Explain.

What was the result of David dwelling on his problem and looking within himself for counsel (v. 2)?

With what two words does David address his request to God (v. 3)?

What does the use of repeated words with similar meanings tell you about David's request?

Have you noticed how God responds to our most desperate prayers? Why does it seem like God responds to our desperation more readily than our surface, everyday prayers?

In his request, what does David recognize about his sight?

Our feelings are not wrong. They are a gift from God and can offer valuable information about us. The problem is that our feelings operate in a fallen state, therefore we cannot trust our feelings alone. When we submit them to Christ, He will help us discern truth and remind us of His faithfulness.

What happened when David turned and submitted his feelings to God (v. 5–6)?

David's longing for God met his lament of what was wrong in the world that should be right. He mourned the injustice. He grieved his enemy's sin deeply. He wept and wailed in the wilderness. When he dwelt on it, he could not carry its weight. Yet when he turned it over to God, he emerged from his despair trusting and rejoicing.

What are you desperate for? What injustice or grievance are you carrying? Are you emotionally spent? Talk to God about it. He honors your laments. He hears your cries. Trust Him. Surrender. Consider adding this to your confession.

Father, I come before Your throne believing Your promise that I am Yours. You have chosen me and called me Your own. Lord, I confess that life does not always feel fair. Its weight is sometimes too great to bear. Yet when I turn it over to You, You lift the burden and fill me with Your love. You cause my heart to rejoice because I trust in You. Thank You for caring about my lament. Help me continually surrender my burdens to You. In Jesus' name, amen.

You will seek me and find me, when you seek me with all your heart.
Jeremiah 29:13

Day Five
Seeking God in the Wilderness

Check Your Posture: Open your hands and heart, and pray Psalm 139:23–24:

> *Search me, O God, and know my heart! Try me and know my thoughts! And see if there be any grievous way in me, and lead me in the way everlasting!*

Ponder and Personalized Practice

> *My son, if you receive my words and treasure up my commandments with you, making your ear attentive to wisdom and inclining your heart to understanding; yes, if you call out for insight and raise your voice for understanding, if you seek it like silver and search for it as for hidden treasures, then you will understand the fear of the Lord and find the knowledge of God.*
>
> Proverbs 2:1–5

When I was a young adult, I recall losing a pair of sunglasses that I had spent more money on than I had spent on any other accessory. As a financially poor young adult, it felt like a major loss. I scoured my house with a sense of urgency, searching high and low for my sunglasses. Although they are long gone now, I eventually found them.

Can you think of a valuable item you have lost and searched for with a sense of urgency? Write it down.

I want to ask you the question I asked myself after losing those sunglasses. Do you search Scripture and seek wisdom, knowledge, and understanding with the same urgency as that possession?

Now consider what Proverbs 2:1–5 says: "If you seek it (wisdom and understanding) like silver and search for it as for hidden treasures, then you will understand the fear of the Lord and find the knowledge of God."

Ponder: If we are not seeking God with that same sense of urgency, we need to take an honest look at why that is.

Where do you need to trust God more in your life? Ask the Lord to show you now. Then ask God to stir the thirst within you for Him alone. Add this to your confession.

As we close this week, remember Jesus is our living water through the wilderness. Seek Him like a hidden treasure — with urgency — and you will find peace and satisfaction in Him.

Practice: Do you sense an urgency that God may be prompting in you? Talk to God about that. As you reflect on it over the weekend, jot down any revelation God reveals. What is one step you can take today toward that action?

I cannot wait for next week's focus where we will examine how turning to God causes us to remember His unfailing faithfulness and to meditate on His promises.

Father, *You are the well of living water. I thirst for You alone. You are the well of my salvation. Fill me. Quench my thirst. And cause me to thirst again until I am complete in Your love. Thank You that when I seek You, Your promise is that I will know the fear of the Lord and find the knowledge of God. Help me to continually seek You like a hidden treasure today and every day. In Jesus' name, amen.*

With joy you will draw water from the wells of salvation.

Isaiah 12:3

Scripture Informed Revelation

My child,

I love when you earnestly seek Me; when you awake early or stay up just a little later to seek My face. I hear you even when you have no words. When grief runs deep, My Spirit groans utterances too deep for words, interceding in unison with your ache. Seek Me. Thirst for Me. Desire Me. Child, I hear your cry when words cannot pierce the surface of this deep, deep well.

Guttural groans, soul crouched low, the body has fallen into a fetal position, weeping. I see you. Never stop seeking Me. For I am working in the dry and desolate places of your soul. I will make a way. I am the Way.

My Spirit never stops groaning over the suffering in this world. Keep praying and seeking, for this is only temporary.

Jeremiah 29:13
Hebrews 11:6
John 14:6
Romans 8:26-28
Psalm 56:8
2 Corinthians 4:17-18
1 Thessalonians 5:16-18
Psalm 30:5

Week Three

A Posture of Presence

"The mind feasts on what it focuses on. What consumes my thinking will be the making or the breaking of my identity."[11]
Uninvited: Living Loved When You Feel Less Than, Left Out, and Lonely
Lysa Terkeurst

---

[11] Terkeurst, Lysa. *Uninvited: Living Loved When You Feel Less Than, Left Out, and Lonely*. Nelson Books, Nashville, Tennessee, 2016, pp. 29.

Day One
Remember God's Power and Glory

Check Your Posture: Open your hands and heart, and pray Psalm 139:23–24:

> *Search me, O God, and know my heart! Try me and know my thoughts! And see if there be any grievous way in me, and lead me in the way everlasting!*

Devotional
Replacing Lies with Truth

> *I have looked upon you in the sanctuary, beholding your power and glory.*
>
> Psalm 63:2

> *My soul will be satisfied as with fat and rich food, and my mouth will praise you with joyful lips, when I remember you upon my bed, and meditate on you in the watches of the night.*
>
> Psalm 63:5–6

Are you tired of lies holding you back?

"I'm so sick of it!" I sat upright across from my friend. I was not mad at her. I was acknowledging my frustration over the enemy's crafty lies, causing me to remain stuck and stagnant. I was sick of the devious deceptions the enemy used to convince me my gifts, talents, and personality were not enough.

My friend nodded. "I think you have to get to that point."

Believing the lie, that I needed to offer more than I could give, caused me to repeatedly back down, turn, and run in the other direction. What I failed to recognize was the whole truth.

I can go only so far in my strength, but God promises to carry me through opposition until the work is complete. It is true, I am not strong enough on my own. *But* what God calls me to He will equip me for. He promises He will be with me and carry me through every trial.

When it comes to those wilderness seasons, it is easy to forget God's promises. Observe the Israelites in the wilderness. A journey that could have taken them eight days to reach the Promised Land took forty years because God's people did not trust His promise—that He would fight their battles and give them the land of milk and honey. I can relate to the cycle of trusting, questioning, and wandering repeatedly. Can you?

After the exodus, the first generation of Israelites failed to enter the Promised Land because they chronically complained, doubted, and shrank back in fear. Yet God's promises are for the believing, a land of faith for people of faith.

Do you feel like you've been wandering a lifetime in the wilderness, waiting for what God has put on your heart? Does something God has called you to feel out of reach? Have you lacked the faith that God's strength will carry you through?

David experienced this too. After his anointing as the next king of Israel, he waited approximately twenty years, during which he spent approximately ten years fleeing Saul in the wilderness of Judah. The difference is that David's trust in God's promises never wavered. He understood his need for God amidst desperation. God used the time of wilderness to draw David to Himself, which better prepared him for his anointing.

In Psalm 63, David grieved his enemies' pursuit and mourned the injustice of all the wrong in his world. He wept and wailed in the wilderness. However, David turned his lament over to God, focusing on truth rather than dwelling on present circumstances. This is a powerful weapon that you and I also have access to.

In Psalm 63:2 and 5–6, we sense David's weariness dissipating after desiring God's presence with insatiable thirst in the wilderness of Judah. From longing for God to meditating on Him, David experienced strength and deep satisfaction simply by remembering his encounters with God.

I have looked upon you in the sanctuary, beholding your power and glory (v. 2).

My soul will be satisfied as with fat and rich food, and my mouth will praise you with joyful lips, when I remember you upon my bed, and meditate on you in the watches of the night (v. 5–6).

The Psalm does not reveal the period between the events of Psalm 63. The cycle of David's grief, longing, and deep satisfaction likely repeated itself over the years. The point is that he turned to God. God honors our grief. We can linger in our laments as we wrestle with and seek God. In these troubling times, He will give us the strength to carry on with a heart of praise, as we recall his faithfulness.

Like the Israelites gathering enough manna for each day, David gained daily strength in the early mornings or late nights when he meditated on God.

We, too, can rest in God's presence when we seek communion with Him through remembering His faithfulness and meditating on the truths of His Word.

Are you ready to call out the lies rolling around your mind? When have you trusted God with a sense of hope, then quickly questioned Him in discouragement? Pay attention to what makes you feel like you are aimlessly wandering. Is there a lie rolling around that you have believed? Name it. Then earnestly bring it to God and let Him replace it with truth.

Because lies only hold the power we give them.

For Further Application: Consider whether you are in a wilderness season or remember the last time you were in one. What promises of God can you cling to, or have you clung to?

Father, You are faithful to keep Your promises. I confess that I forget far too often how good You are. Thank You for leaving a record of Your faithfulness in Scripture and one to create in our lives. This matters for remembering Your power and glory and the promises to come. Help me to remember all the ways You have been faithful so I may trust You more fully with my future. Help me to trust that You will equip me for what You call me to. In Jesus' name, amen.

> *Jesus said to them, "I am the bread of life; whoever comes to me shall not hunger, and whoever believes in me shall never thirst."*
>
> John 6:35

Day Two
Cultivating a Desire for God
Remembering

Check Your Posture: Open your hands and heart, and pray Psalm 139:23–24:
Search me, O God, and know my heart! Try me and know my thoughts! And see if there be any grievous way in me, and lead me in the way everlasting!

Commentary, Part One:

We are forgetful, but God is faithful.

I remember the morning I snuggled into the living room couch, working through the homework for a weekly Bible study on the patriarchs. I was reading about the Israelites' grumbling and complaining immediately after witnessing miracles. I felt merciless disdain over their forgetfulness. I asked aloud why God had given them so many chances. That was when it hit me. *Gasp!*

"That is me, isn't it, Lord? I have been just like the Israelites, believing one day and doubting the next. But You, Lord, have always been merciful with me." It is a sobering realization we all come to in our faith walk. The experience of the Israelites in the wilderness reminds us of our humanity. Yet David's contemplations in the wilderness of Judah teach us a valuable lesson in trust.

David beheld God's glory, hovering above the Ark of the Covenant in the Holy of Holies of the Tabernacle. He encountered God's power in the sanctuary. When Saul drove David from this holy place to the wilderness, he felt the loss. He felt distant from God without the physical manifestations before him. Unlike the Israelites, however, David did not grumble in his lament. Instead, he recounted God's power and glory that he had witnessed in the sanctuary.

The Hebrew meaning of sanctuary defines it as a holy or consecrated place.[12] *Webster's Dictionary 1828*[13] also defines it as a place of refuge and safety.

David's contemplations of God in the sanctuary soon equated to the reality of God's presence in the wilderness, not by any physical manifestation of God, but by faith. David learned that the sanctuary is not a specific locality. It is wherever a soul deeply thirsts for God.

In the wilderness of Judah, exposed to the elements and pursued by

---

[12] "H6944 - qōdeš - Strong's Hebrew Lexicon (kjv)." Blue Letter Bible. Web. 8 March, 2023 <https://www.blueletterbible.org/lexicon/h6944/kjv/wlc/ss0/0-1>.

[13] https://webstersdictionary1828.com/Dictionary/sanctuar–

his enemies for years, David found refuge in God Himself.

Remembering who God is and His faithfulness infuses our faith to believe big. It is key to inhabiting the promised land — the places of our purpose and anointing.

We may be forgetful, but God is faithful. We only need to turn and behold Him.

Questions

Read Psalm 27:4. What is the one thing David desires of the LORD?

What does he see and wish to do in this space?

What is the result (v. 5)?

Do you think David's desire is limited to the physical temple (see 1 Cor. 6:19)? Explain.

Have you ever felt like you could not wait to be in God's presence and experience His beauty? When we experience God's presence, we never want to leave. Yet when life gets busy, we forget. Can you relate? This is why we must create space to remember God's goodness and seek His presence, regardless of our feelings or circumstances.

Read Psalm 62:7–8. What does the psalmist implore the people to do?

Share ways that help you remember God is your salvation and refuge. Write down one daily habit you can implement to help you remember to seek Him.

Father, *we are forgetful, but You are faithful. I confess I can be like the Israelites who forgot Your wonders and grumbled through change. Thank You for being faithful in fulfilling Your promises regardless. Help me to have a heart like David's, who turned to You in his grief and recounted Your power and glory. Help me to trust You with a deep reverence like David displayed in the wilderness. Help me to trust You with what You call me to. In Jesus' name, amen.*

But we are not of those who shrink back and are destroyed, but of those who have faith and preserve their souls.

Hebrews 10:39

Day Three
Promises

Check Your Posture: Open your hands and heart, and pray Psalm 139:23–24:

> *Search me, O God, and know my heart! Try me and know my thoughts! And see if there be any grievous way in me, and lead me in the way everlasting!*

Soak, Scripture, and Scribble

Soak: Search and listen to the song, "Promises," by Maverick City Music, while resting in God's presence.

Going deeper: consider standing. Close your eyes and sense God leading your posture in His presence.

(Soak)

Scripture focus: Psalm 135, 136

When we turn to God, He reminds us of the promise that He is good and always with us. I'm so thankful for His faithfulness. Are you?

Questions

Read Psalm 135. Notice the heart's response of the psalmist in Psalm 135 when recounting what God has done.

How does the psalmist honor God before he accounts for what God has done?

Name some events the psalmist recounts.

How does the psalmist conclude his song?

Read Psalm 136. What is our proper response to who God is and what He has done?

Is the psalmist's praise fueled by emotion or reason? Explain.

Scribble: Consider a challenging time God brought you through. Think of the ways He has been faithful to you through trials. Create a timeline highlighting His faithfulness, then follow the pattern of Psalm 135 to write this prayer from your own story.

Include praise, ways God has been faithful, and an exhortation for others to bless the Lord. Add this to your confession.

Father, I praise You because You are good. You have drawn me out of my pit and into Your loving care. Your name is pleasant. You have chosen me to be yours. You have made all things by the word of Your mouth. Thank You for Your great faithfulness to me. Help me to always recount Your faithfulness and trust in Your promises over my life. You are a good Father. I am Yours. In Jesus' name, amen.

Know therefore that the LORD your God is God, the faithful God who keeps covenant and steadfast love with those who love him and keep his commandments, to a thousand generations.

Deuteronomy 7:9

Day Four
Cultivating a Desire for God
Meditating

Check Your Posture: Open your hands and heart, and pray Psalm 139:23–24:

> *Search me, O God, and know my heart! Try me and know my thoughts! And see if there be any grievous way in me, and lead me in the way everlasting!*

Commentary, Part Two:

Consider a time when you were so hungry the anticipation of food made your mouth water. Recalling our favorite food deepens our hunger and longing for it. Like being thirsty and desperate for water, we will not stop thinking about our hunger until it is satisfied. It is one thing to remember the foods we desire and another to feast on them. When we indulge, our hunger is satisfied.

This is what David experienced in the wilderness of Judah when he meditated on God through the watches of the night.

David did not just remember who God was, he meditated on Him. To remember is to call something to mind. To meditate is to think deeply about it and focus on it for an extended period. Where remembering God's glory identifies our longing for God Himself, meditating on Him satisfies that longing.

Scripture often identifies Jesus with food. Have you thought about why? The reference to bread, banquets, and feasts; the reference to our thirst and hunger; the invitation to taste Him for ourselves. When Psalm 63:5–6 states that David will be satisfied like fat and rich foods when he meditates on God throughout the night watches, it means he is feasting on the marrow of God Himself.

Psalm 23:5 describes this allegory well: *You prepare a table before me in the presence of my enemies; you anoint my head with oil; my cup overflows.*

In this passage, we see a beautiful illustration of someone who has taken time to prepare a meal for another person. This is intimate. It is a meal for one even amongst his enemies. God does not eliminate life's trials or our enemies before offering the meal prepared for us. God spreads a lavish feast before us amidst our trials and amongst our enemies.

David feasted on God's lavish love in the night watches of the wilderness. He declared his soul overflowing with satisfaction and joy with every remembrance and meditation on Him. This is where David found peace and rest. In fact, David received more rest while meditating on God throughout the night than with a full night's sleep.

Remembering God is calling to mind the lavish foods we hunger for. Meditating on Him is to dig in and feast on them. This is where we will find our rest, no matter where we are or what battle we face.

The table is ready. Your place is set. Will you come?

Questions

Read John 6:35. How does Jesus identify Himself?

Read Luke 14:15-24. This parable titled, "The Messiah's Banquet," is also referred to as "The Marriage Supper of the Lamb," based on Revelation 19:9. What is the point of this parable?

For what two reasons do people choose not to come to this great feast? (v. 18-20)?

What circumstances might these excuses represent for us in our faith walk?

Why do you think there is urgency in the master's command to fill the house (v. 21-23)?

In biblical times, it was an honor to receive an invitation like this. The time of the feast was not determined in advance only the day itself. The people would come when summoned. Not to come was a grave insult after all that had been prepared in advance.

Consider when you accepted Christ's invitation. What did that look like?

How can excuses keep us from receiving all that God has prepared for us?

How can we best honor God with the invitation we have accepted?

Father, *You are good. You intimately prepare a table before me. You invite me to come and feast on all that You have prepared for me. You fill me with complete satisfaction. Why would I not come? Search my heart and know me. Show me any unclean spirit within me and lead me always to the path of righteousness and Your everlasting banquet table. In Jesus' name, amen.*

> *He brought me to the banqueting house, and his banner over me was love.*
>
> Song of Solomon 2:4

Day Five
Getting Radical in the Wilderness

Check Your Posture: Open your hands and heart, and pray Psalm 139:23–24:

> *Search me, O God, and know my heart! Try me and know my thoughts! And see if there be any grievous way in me, and lead me in the way everlasting!*

Ponder and Personalized Practice

> *Even though I walk through the valley of the shadow of death, I will fear no evil, for you are with me; And your rod and your staff, they comfort me.*
>
> Psalm 23:4

David was radical. He sought God to the point there was no room in his heart and mind for distracting shadows. His enemies sought his life, yet he never feared how they might take him down. Instead, he asked God to handle them. Although David felt fear like we all feel, he spoke truth into the wilderness of his soul. Psalm 23 has another powerful passage reflecting David's posture: *The LORD is my shepherd ... I will fear no evil* (Ps. 23:1, 4).

David did not doubt God's anointing in his life. His grief led him into deeper communion with God.

Although death may be a shadow tempting to distract us with fear, the Good Shepherd protects us. Fixing our eyes on Him and meditating on the truth of His redemption will overshadow the enemy every time.

If getting radical means leaving no room for the enemy's distractions, then it's time to get radical about Jesus!

I cannot wait to dive into next week with you when we explore David's praise in the wilderness. As we find true satisfaction in God's presence, our natural response is praise.

Ponder: As we close this week, feast on Jesus through prayer, worship, and meditation on His Word. My prayer is that you will be satisfied. The table has been prepared and set before you. Feast on the goodness of God.

Practice: Depending on the weather, take a walk. As you walk, relax, and breathe deeply. Inhale the air and your surroundings. Recall moments of God's grace and faithfulness. What memory comes to your mind? Record this after your walk.

Optional: Refresh your memory of God's faithfulness to David by reading aloud, writing, or memorizing Psalm 23.

Write the Psalm here:

Father, *You are my Shepherd. I do not need to fear evil, for You will protect me. Although I may experience trials, no harm will befall me. Death does not have the final say because You have defeated death. Thank You for this victory! Help me to trust You through the trials and any healing needed in my life. Help me to trust You so radically that the enemy has no grip on my life. In Jesus' name, amen.*

> *Jesus said to them, 'I am the bread of life; whoever comes to me shall not hunger, and whoever believes in me shall never thirst.*
>
> John 6:35

Scripture Informed Revelation

Dear one,

I am ever present. Even when you feel abandoned and alone, I am near. Turn to Me. Remember when you were unsure if you could face another morning? Then the sun rose, and new mercies renewed your hope for another day. My presence is where you will find all you need for this journey. Day by day, I lead you.

I lead you through the wilderness on the right path.

I lead you through tumultuous emotions to still waters.

I lead you through unrest to places of peace.

I lead you through scarcity to a banquet set before you.

I lead you from the desolate valley to green pastures.

I lead you to the Highway that is the only Way to the abundant life I have promised you.

In Me, you have the fullness of life. In My presence, you are whole.

Psalm 34:18
James 4:8-10
Lamentations 3:22-23
Psalm 23
Isaiah 35:8
Psalm 16:11

Week Four

A Posture of Praise

"It is the true believer only who will bless the Lord when he takes away his gifts or hides his face."[14]

The Treasury of David, Charles Spurgeon

---

[14] Spurgeon, Charles. *The Treasury of David: The Complete Seven Volumes. Vol. 3,* E-book Ed., 2012, pp.1881.

Day One
Praise God No Matter the Circumstance

Check Your Posture: Open your hands and heart, and pray Psalm 139:23–24:

> *Search me, O God, and know my heart! Try me and know my thoughts! And see if there be any grievous way in me, and lead me in the way everlasting!*

Devotional
Praise as a Pleasing Sacrifice

> *Because your steadfast love is better than life, my lips will praise you. So I will bless you as long as I live; in your name will I lift up my hands. My soul will be satisfied as with fat and rich food, and my mouth will praise you with joyful lips, when I remember you upon my bed, and meditate on you in the watches of the night.*
>
> Psalm 63:3–6

How deeply does praise permeate your life?

I am no stranger to praise in various expressions. Since childhood and throughout the years, I have witnessed or participated in singing, shouting, lifting hands, kneeling, clapping, dancing, marching, jumping, and falling to one's face. On the other hand, I know that everyone struggles with sin and brokenness (even Christians who praise the Lord) and can appear hypocritical. I have wondered how to reconcile this contradiction.

Without realizing it, I began to question genuine praise and even doubted its sincerity in others' lives and my own.

When it came to writing about praise for this study, I paused. Frankly, I started writing this devotional a few years ago but then set it aside. I questioned my understanding of how genuine praise helps us pursue Christ's victory in our lives. I've been studying and praying about it ever since.

Praise is an outward expression of honor due to God simply because of His nature. Seven different Hebrew words and their expressions throughout Scripture define it, not just one![15] It is like our battle cry in a spiritual war waging around us. Yet I have found that the outward expression of praise fluently flows from an inward transformation (Pr. 4:23). We can sing, shout, and stomp our way to the victory Christ already secured for us, however, we will not sustain a proper posture of praise nor

---

[15] Worship: The 7 Hebrew Words of Praise - Logos Sermons

trust the victory to be ours without the Holy Spirit permeating our hearts through and through.

We cannot assume this inward transformation or take it for granted just because we call ourselves Christian. Christians are targets for the enemy. We, of all people, need the sword of the Spirit and the full armor of God (Ephesians 6) as we act in our callings.

Psalm 63 portrays David's spiritual defense as a genuine, unabashed sacrifice of praise. The Hebrew word for sacrifice, often used in the Psalms, is *zābah*, meaning to kill, offer, or slay.[16] God required the ancient Israelites to slay an unblemished animal as an offering. This would demonstrate turning from their sin to draw near God's presence. Today, Jesus is the ultimate sacrifice, the unblemished lamb who died on the cross for our sins. Instead of an altar, we have the cross. We no longer kill an animal but slay our will to draw near to God. An offering of genuine praise is a pleasing sacrifice to Him.

God desires our praise to be constant in the way He desires our trust. Four out of the eleven verses in Psalm 63 articulate David's outward expression of praise. David's life was on the line, yet he was more desperate to experience God's presence than to save his own life.

Because your steadfast love is better than life, my lips will praise you (v. 3).
So I will bless you as long as I live; in your name will I lift up my hands (v. 4).
My soul will be satisfied as with fat and rich food and my mouth will praise you with joyful lips (v. 5).
For you have been my help, and in the shadow of your wings I will sing for joy (v. 7).

Do we praise in the desperate times, as well as the joyful times? Do we desire God's presence in our lives more than life itself? Praise may be our defense, the Word of God our weapon, and we can arm ourselves as Ephesians 6 describes the full armor of God. However, the only way to fight with these vital elements is with a humble and contrite spirit, like David's (Ps. 51:17). We must begin with a posture of humility and allow the Holy Spirit to infuse our praise with His presence.

Are you honest and vulnerable with the hard, uncomfortable stuff? We cannot only strive for the mountaintops without trusting God through the valleys. What will it take to trust your Savior today? Trust Him with your complaints, your grief, your frustration, your disappointment, your doubt, and your fear. Be still and know that He is God. Recall the ways He

---

[16] "H2076 - zābaḥ - Strong's Hebrew Lexicon (kjv)." Blue Letter Bible. Web. 9 April, 2023. <https://www.blueletterbible.org/lexicon/h2076/kjv/wlc/0-1/>.

is faithful. Allow Him to work in the deep, secret places of your soul. Let your praise be the work of the Holy Spirit permeating every aspect of your life.

Our praise is a pleasing sacrifice when it displays our complete trust and obedience in God. In what area is God challenging you to trust Him today?

For Further Application: Compare and contrast 2 Samuel 5:19-20 and 2 Samuel 11:1-5. What is the difference in David's spiritual posture and what were the outcomes? How can you apply this to your life?

Heavenly Father, You are worthy of all praise. No storm I face is too great for You. You are awesome and trustworthy. As I seek You, You are kind to show me your goodness and steadfast love. My response is gratitude and praise. Thank You that I can praise You in the middle of my storm and feel at peace. May my praise be pleasing to You. May it be infused with trust and obedience. May I draw near to You through this offering. You are worthy. In Jesus' name, amen

> *Let my prayer be counted as incense before you, and the lifting up of my hands as the evening sacrifice!*
> Psalm 141:2

Day Two
Cultivating a Heart of Praise
The Work of Our Whole Lives

Check Your Posture: Open your hands and heart, and pray Psalm 139:23–24:

> *Search me, O God, and know my heart! Try me and know my thoughts!*
> *And see if there be any grievous way in me, and lead me in the way*
> *everlasting!*

Commentary, Part One:

Should we save praise for Sunday?

My family and I recently returned from Juarez, Mexico, where a team built a 16x18' house for a multi-generational family with the organization, Casas Por Cristo. The family previously lived in a cinderblock dwelling half the size with dirt floors and blankets overtop as a roof. A small bedroom in your home is bigger than that. The poverty in Juarez is no doubt a hardship. Yet the children running around our building site seemed unfazed by it. They were curious and full of life. They giggled and played like the outdoors was their canvas of delight. They did not appear to notice the monochromatic scheme of desert browns with trash scattered in every direction. They contained a joy that was not dependent on the luxuries or comforts of this world.

When we handed over the keys to the $10,000 home we had just built, the family witnessed a miracle before their eyes. They could never have afforded this house in their lifetime. Gratitude welled within their hearts and spilled into words of praise and expressions of thankfulness. They smothered us with long, tight hugs, deeply and genuinely moved to a heart overwhelmed by God's provision.

True praise is not something we conjure up. It is the work of our lives and deeply felt through a heart of gratitude. One that surrenders to God. Surrender is letting go of our resistance and yielding completely to God. Through surrender, God stirs our hearts to praise.

The practice of gratitude we often hear about, reducing anxiety and enhancing our health and relationships, is simply the result of our surrender. It is the practice of yielding our hearts to God, experiencing His presence, and acknowledging His provisions, even through our struggles. It is opening our eyes to witness God's splendid beauty, even in the monotonous spaces of our lives.

In the monochromatic spaces of David's desert wanderings, God worked this kind of delight out in him. He transformed David's deep desire for God and surrender into a heart full of praise. David completed his enjoyment of God by singing hymns, lifting his hands to heaven, and joyfully blessing Him. Similarly, a heartfelt hug and joyful commending completed the feeling of gratitude in the family receiving their new home in Juarez, Mexico. Praise is more than a feeling. It is an outward expression that completes the feeling.

In *Reflections on the Psalms*, by C.S. Lewis, Lewis describes this beautifully. "It is in the process of being worshiped that God communicates His presence to men."[17] God desires our praise through adoration and thanksgiving, not because He is self-absorbed, but because it is one way He communicates the delight of His presence to us.

With surrendered hearts, God invites us to fully enjoy Him by glorifying Him daily. His invitation is meant for more than our Sunday service. True praise is the work of our whole lives.

Pause and consider what it means for you to glorify and enjoy God.

Questions

Read Psalm 67. Verse 1 comes from Numbers 6:24–26, where the high priest professed this beautiful blessing over the people. What three requests did the Psalmists make?

According to Psalm 67:2, what purpose did the Psalmist make his requests?

How does the purpose for God's generous blessing in this prayer affect your perspective on receiving blessings from God?

According to verses 3 through 5, what does the Psalmist desire the people to do? For what reason?

How many times does the Psalmist repeat this desire in these verses?

---

[17] Lewis, C.S. *Reflections on the Psalms*. William Collins, Glasgow, Scotland, 2020, pp.108.

What do you think is the significance of his repetition?

What tense is the Psalmist praying in? Is he referring to the past, present, or future when praying for the people?

In verses 4 and 6, the King James Version gives the reasons for his request in the future tense:

> *For thou shalt judge the people righteously...* (v. 4)

> *Then shall the earth yield her increase...* (v. 6a)

Consider the relationship between cause and effect in this chapter. When will God bless us?

The Psalmist repeats twice that God will bless us in verses 6 and 7. How does the Psalmist reference God in verse 6b? How is this significant to you?

How does the cause and effect of praise (glorifying God) and blessing (enjoying the fruit of God's increase) impact you in your life? Can we separate them and they still have their intended purpose?

Summarize in one or two sentences the connection between praise (glorifying God) and blessing (enjoying God), according to Psalm 67.

Lord, I glorify Your name. Your name is above all names. You are my provider and protector. Your love overwhelms me. The life You have given me is reason enough to praise You. The sun rising and setting is enough reason to praise You. Your loving-kindness is enough reason to praise You. The cross is enough reason to praise You. I confess I take these everyday gifts for granted. Thank You for Your provision in my life. Help me to always see the little ways You love and care for Your children. You are so good to me. In Jesus' name, amen.

> *For this I will praise you, O LORD, among the nations, and sing praises to your name.*
>
> 2 Samuel 22:50

Day Three
Gratitude

Check Your Posture: Open your hands and heart, and pray Psalm 139:23–24:

> *Search me, O God, and know my heart! Try me and know my thoughts!*
> *And see if there be any grievous way in me, and lead me in the way*
> *everlasting!*

Soak, Scripture, and Scribble

Soak: Search and listen to the song, "Gratitude," by Maverick City, while resting in God's presence.

Going deeper: Consider standing in God's presence. If led, throw up your hands in complete abandon.

(Soak)

Scripture Focus: Hebrews 13:15

Through surrender to God's Word and ways, we abide in Christ, and by Him flows our praise. Think about feeling in awe when a baby coos or when you witness a sunrise. There is wonder in our gaze because of the miracle we witness. As believers, we understand it is not by us or anything we did that we stand in awe. It is *by God*.

Hebrews 13:15 tells us that *God* fills us with wonder and praise, and through our surrender we continually, sacrificially, and outwardly express that praise. God alone makes our praise pleasing to Him possible. It is our abiding in Christ through prayer, reflection, and meditation on what He has already done, and absolute trust in what He says He will do. This is an incredible grace. Have you experienced this grace?

Questions

Consider proper praise in your life:

> *By him therefore let us offer the sacrifice of praise to God continually,*
> *that is, the fruit of our lips giving thanks to his name.*
> Hebrews 13:15, KJV

By him –
Read 1 Timothy 2:5–6. Based on this passage, how is our praise *by* God?

Continually –
Read 1 Thessalonians 5:18. When and how often does this passage say to give thanks?

Costly or Sacrificially –
Read Psalm 51:17. When does this passage say praise is costly or sacrificial?

Outward expression –
Read Psalm 63:4–7 again. What are the ways David expresses or professes to express his praise?

Looking again at Hebrews 13:15, how is our continual and sacrificial outward expression of genuine praise made possible?

Scribble: What are you going through right now? Consider the challenging time God brought you through that you wrote about last week. Scribble your praise to Him for bringing you through it and for what you trust He will do in your current circumstance based on His character. Feel free to draw or write your praise. Add this to your confession.

Pray Psalm 135:1–3 with me:

Praise the LORD!

Praise the name of the LORD,
give praise, O servants of the LORD,
who stand in the house of the LORD,
In the courts of the house of our God!
Praise the LORD, for the LORD is good;
Sing to his name, for it is pleasant!

Lord, *I know my praise alone is not much, but it is enough when I surrender my heart. It is enough when I trust in who You are, what You have done, and what You have promised to do. Thank You for being the same yesterday, today, and forever. Help me to trust You so I may continually praise You. In Jesus' name, amen.*

I will bless the LORD at all times: his praise shall continually be in my mouth.

Psalm 34:1

Day Four
Cultivating a Heart of Praise
Our Response

Check Your Posture: Open your hands and heart, and pray Psalm 139:23–24:

> *Search me, O God, and know my heart! Try me and know my thoughts! And see if there be any grievous way in me, and lead me in the way everlasting!*

Commentary, Part Two:

How do we praise through the wilderness?

When my firstborn wobbled his first steps toward me and fell into my arms, everyone around him raised their hands and voices in emphatic praise. My son rejoiced with us, ready to try again. When trying again, he giggled and responded joyfully before starting because he trusted the process even more. He trusted my voice and that I would catch his fall as he lunged into me. For my new toddler, trust meant everything in taking those first steps with his eyes fixed on me. He responded to my call and rejoiced in response to my praise.

When we remember God's character through what He has done and trust His voice for what He will do, like a parent's voice, praise will be our natural response.

In Psalm 63:3, David attunes his ear to God's voice to the point he recognizes his spiritual life in God's presence as better than his temporal life as king. All the pleasures and comforts of life that are ahead mean nothing to him compared to God's everlasting love and mercy. What a sweet place to be when waiting on God through an enduring wilderness. David's response to his deep sense of satisfaction is a caress toward heaven with raised arms and joyful lips.

According to *Strong's Concordance*, David's response of praise in Psalm 63:3 comes from the Hebrew word *sabah* and means to address in a loud tone, to reach out with affection for God, to feel his hold on us, to commend: *Because your steadfast love is better than life, my lips will praise you.*[18]

David's expression of praise here is intimate, enthusiastic, and anchored in trust.

David also prophesied in the wilderness other expressions of praise throughout his life, trusting that God would see him through his

---

[18] "H7623 - šāḇaḥ - Strong's Hebrew Lexicon (kjv)." Blue Letter Bible. Web. 23 April, 2023. <https://www.blueletterbible.org/lexicon/h7623/kjv/wlc/0-1/>.

circumstances.

In Psalm 63:4, the Hebrew word for "bless" is *barak*, meaning to kneel: *So I will bless you as long as I live; in your name will I lift up my hands.*[19]

This form of praise shows David's sincere reverence for God.

In Psalm 63:5, the Hebrew word for praise is *halal*, meaning to shine; hence, to make a show, to boast; and thus, to be (clamorously) foolish; to rave; causatively, to celebrate: *My soul will be satisfied as with fat and rich food and my mouth will praise you with joyful lips.*[20]

David anticipates a satisfaction so rich in God, his response is unadulterated praise.

There is not just one way to express our praise. There are seven expressions in Scripture compatible with different circumstances. Sometimes we kneel, other times we dance. Sometimes we sing, other times we shout. The deeper our trust in suffering, the louder our praise will be when satisfied by God.

When surrender anchors our trust like David's, gratitude can overwhelm our hearts and overflow into an outward expression of praise—no matter how dire our circumstances.

Questions

Read Psalm 63:5–7. When does this passage say David will praise God?

What does David recall that encourages his praise?

Read Isaiah 25. For what reason does Isaiah praise in verses 1–5?

In verse 6, Isaiah moves from the past tense to the future tense, describing the marriage supper on Mount Zion when the fullness of God's salvation comes for all people. Notice the rich food full of marrow described. How

---

[19] "H1288 - bārak - Strong's Hebrew Lexicon (kjv)." Blue Letter Bible. Web. 23 April, 2023. <https://www.blueletterbible.org/lexicon/h1288/kjv/wlc/0-1/>.
[20] "H1984 - hālal - Strong's Hebrew Lexicon (kjv)." Blue Letter Bible. Web. 23 April, 2023. <https://www.blueletterbible.org/lexicon/h1984/kjv/wlc/0-1/>.

does Psalm 63:5 compare to the marriage supper described in Isaiah 25:6? What does this comparison say about David's ongoing satisfaction in God?

According to verses 7–9, why do we always have reason to praise (see also Philippians 1:6)?

Name the reasons given to praise in the following verses:

Isaiah 43:1

John 3:16

Ephesians 2:8–9

Romans 6:23

Read Psalm 100:4–5. Name the reason this passage gives to praise God today and always.

Based on these verses, should our praise be a response to our circumstances or to who God is, what He has done, and promises to do?

   Father, You are glorious. You are my safe fortress, redeemer, and King. I have reason to praise You every single day! Lord, I confess that I don't always feel like praising You. Yet when I enter Your presence with a surrendered heart, You work it out in me. Thank You for how You love me and call me Your own. Help me to praise You always, my King and my God. In Jesus' name, amen.

Enter his gates with thanksgiving, and his courts with praise! Give thanks to him; bless his name!

Psalm 100:4

Day Five
Genuine Praise Through the Wilderness

Check Your Posture: Open your hands and heart, and pray Psalm 139:23–24:

> *Search me, O God, and know my heart! Try me and know my thoughts! And see if there be any grievous way in me, and lead me in the way everlasting!*

Ponder and Personalized Practice

> *And Mary said, 'My soul magnifies the Lord and my spirit rejoices in God my Savior, for he has looked on the humble estate of his servant. For behold, from now on all generations will call me blessed; for he who is mighty has done great things for me, and holy is his name.'*
>
> Luke 1:46–49

God recognizes genuine praise in a broken and contrite heart.

Mary's praise is a beautiful example of genuine praise. She shows us in her song that God looks upon the humble. It is the humble He draws near to and anoints for a greater purpose. It is the humble who recognizes the wonderful things He has done and trusts Him for what He will do. It is the humble person who genuinely believes and finds reason to praise.

Notice the contrast between David and Saul, both anointed kings of Israel. Saul sought power for himself, while David humbly desired and sought the Lord. Saul's praise was circumstantial. David praised God no matter his circumstances. Because Saul disobeyed God, God removed His anointing. David flourished in his anointing, despite his time in the wilderness.

God desires a broken and contrite spirit because it is where He transforms our hearts and moves us to genuine praise.

Proper praise always precedes victory.

Ponder: What may be holding you back from genuinely praising God? Where does your resistance lie? Take your resistance to Jesus and ask Him to give you a heart of praise. Add these words to your confession.

Practice: Keep a "Gratitude" journal or notepad nearby and record your praise and thanksgiving throughout your weekend. Consider keeping up this practice.

Pray Psalm 145 with me:

> *I will extol you, my God and King,*
> *and bless your name forever and ever.*
> *Every day I will bless you*
> *and praise your name forever and ever.*
> *Great is the Lord, and greatly to be praised,*
> *and his greatness is unsearchable.*
> *One generation shall commend your works to another,*
> *and shall declare your mighty acts.*
> *On the glorious splendor of your majesty,*
> *and on your wondrous works, I will meditate.*
> *They shall speak of the might of your awesome deeds,*
> *and I will declare your greatness.*
> *They shall pour forth the fame of your abundant goodness*
> *and shall sing aloud of your righteousness.*
> *The Lord is gracious and merciful,*
> *slow to anger and abounding in steadfast love.*
> *The Lord is good to all,*
> *and his mercy is over all that he has made.*
> *All your works shall give thanks to you, O Lord,*
> *and all your saints shall bless you!*
> *They shall speak of the glory of your kingdom*
> *and tell of your power,*
> *to make known to the children of man your mighty deeds,*
> *and the glorious splendor of your kingdom.*
> *Your kingdom is an everlasting kingdom,*
> *and your dominion endures throughout all generations.*
> *The Lord is faithful in all his words*
> *and kind in all his works.*
> *The Lord upholds all who are falling*
> *and raises up all who are bowed down.*
> *The eyes of all look to you,*

and you give them their food in due season.
You open your hand;
   you satisfy the desire of every living thing.
The Lord is righteous in all his ways
   and kind in all his works.
The Lord is near to all who call on him,
   to all who call on him in truth.
He fulfills the desire of those who fear him; he also hears their cry and saves them.
The Lord preserves all who love him,
   but all the wicked he will destroy.
My mouth will speak the praise of the Lord, and let all flesh bless his holy name forever and ever.

Lord, *I have so much to be grateful for. I praise You for who You are and how You bestow your goodness to me. Thank You for Your everlasting love, grace, and mercy. In Jesus' name, amen*

Great is the Lord, and greatly to be praised, and his greatness is unsearchable.

Psalm 145:3

Scripture Informed Revelation

Precious one,

You feel the most alive in a posture of praise. This is because it is what I created you for. When you praise Me as Your Creator, you are fully who I created you to be.

When you praise Me, you demonstrate your trust in Me, and I communicate My immeasurable love for you. It is a glorious exchange.

Whether privately or corporately, come with a surrendered heart and I will work My praise in you. Power resounds in your abandoned praise, My child. Come with a humble and contrite heart. Come.

I do not always remove the hardship but reveal My glory through it. Look around. Seek beauty. Seek My face. There is nothing I will not do for the one I have chosen and adore. Open your heart in praise and allow Me to show you who I am.

Come into My presence and find I am your reason for praise.

Psalm 19:1
Psalm 95:6
Revelation 4:11
Isaiah 43:20-21
Psalm 34:1
Acts 16:23-26
Psalm 51:17
1 Peter 1:3-9
Roman's 8:31-32
Psalm 117:1-2

Week Five

A Posture of Surrender

"David had wonderful views of how the everlasting God is Himself the hiding place of the believing soul, and of how He takes the believer and keeps him in the very hollow of His hand, in the secret of His pavilion, under the shadow of His wings, under His very feathers. And there David lived. And oh, we who are the children of Pentecost, we who have known Christ and His blood and the Holy Ghost sent down from heaven, why is it we know so little of what it is to walk tremblingly step by step with the Almighty God as our Keeper?"[21]

Absolute Surrender, Andrew Murray

---

[21] Murray, Andrew. *Absolute Surrender*. B&H Publishing Group, Nashville, Tennessee, 2017, pp.119.

Day One
Cleave to God As Though Your Strength Depends on It

Check Your Posture: Open your hands and heart, and pray Psalm 139:23–24:

> *Search me, O God, and know my heart. Try me and know my thoughts! And see if there be any grievous way in me, and lead me in the way everlasting!*

Devotional
Living Boldly in Christ

> *For you have been my help, and in the shadow of your wings I will sing for joy. My soul clings to you; your right hand upholds me.*
>
> Psalm 63:7–8

How God speaks to our hearts in private is meant to resound in public.

When my husband and I married, our reception celebration felt joyous yet short. Time flies when you're having fun! What I did not understand yet was the strength the intimacy of consecrating our marriage would bring throughout the years. Similarly, our commitment to Christ as we continually surrender to Him will strengthen our bond for the partnership in building His Kingdom.

Psalm 27:5 describes this space where we closely adhere to God as "the secret place of His tabernacle:" *For in the time of trouble He shall hide me in His pavilion; In the secret place of His tabernacle He shall hide me; He shall set me high upon a rock.* (NKJV)

Under the Old Covenant, this "secret place" would have been designated as the Holy of Holies, where God's presence was contained in the Ark of the Covenant and hidden behind the veil. God's presence is our hiding place where He strengthens us for battle, protects us from our enemy, hears our hearts' cries, comforts us with His promises, and reveals revelation to our hearts.

There have been times I laid my head upon my pillow at night when I could not wait for the morning, so I could enter that sweet space with Jesus. No doubt He is with us every minute of the day, but to commune with Him in the secluded space of His heart is to cleave to Him like a bride cleaves to her groom. This space is vital to our faith, the way fellowship and intimacy strengthen the marriage union.

Cleave

The Merriam-Webster Dictionary names common synonyms of cleave:

adhere, cling, cohere, and stick.[22] It states that while all these words mean "to become closely attached," cleave stresses the "strength of attachment."

Furthermore, the word cling used in the English Standard Version of Psalm 63:8 comes from the Hebrew word *dabac*, meaning cling or adhere; figuratively, to catch by pursuit: abide fast, cleave (fast together), follow close (hard after), be joined (together), keep (fast), overtake, pursue hard, stick, take.[23]

It is the Hebrew word we read in Genesis 2:24: *Therefore a man shall leave his father and his mother and hold fast to his wife, and they shall become one flesh.*

For a man to leave the old behind and cling to the new requires a deep trust in the person he has chosen for himself. The result is strength in this sacred covenant. According to one commentary, David Guzik confirms this type of spousal attachment as the partnership and connection the believer experiences with God.[24]

In the wilderness of Judah, David's deep longing for God leads him to experience that secure, sacred covenant. As a result, God holds David securely with his right hand.

God's Right Hand

Throughout Scripture, God's "right hand" symbolizes power. It is not in our power that we press on but in His. God holds us securely in His power so that we may walk in a manner worthy of our calling (Eph. 4:1). David offers a beautiful example of this in his posture of humility and communion with God.

God desires this very connection with you — to hold you securely in His power as you adhere to Him and step out in obedience to His call.

The intimacy we experience in the secret place of God's heart is sacred. He will strengthen and empower us in this space to live our lives boldly for Him.

For Further Application: Consider God's intention for marital intimacy. How do you see this as strengthening a marriage? How can that picture draw you into a better understanding of God's intention for your relationship and secret communion with Him? Jot your thoughts down here.

---

[22] https://www.merriam-webster.com/thesaurus/cleave
[23] "H1692 - dāḇaq - Strong's Hebrew Lexicon (kjv)." Blue Letter Bible. Web. 9 May, 2024. <https://www.blueletterbible.org/lexicon/h1692/kjv/wlc/0-1/>.
[24] Guzik, David. "Study Guide for Psalm 63." Blue Letter Bible. 6/2022. Web. 10 May, 2023. <https://www.blueletterbible.org/comm/guzik_david/study-guide/psalm/psalm-63.cfm>.

Heavenly Father, *You are the one I cling to. I cleave to You today as though my strength depends on it. Admittedly, I often forget that You have promised to go before me, but You are gracious to draw me back to Yourself. You are merciful and kind. Thank You for Your enduring love. Thank You for Your presence. Help me to desire You more than anything and to continue to cling to You all my days. In Jesus' name, amen.*

> *But when you pray, go into your room and shut the door and pray to your Father who is in secret. And your Father who sees in secret will reward you.*
>
> Matthew 6:6

Day Two
Learning to Depend Fully on God
What it Means to Cleave

Check Your Posture: Open your hands and heart, and pray Psalm 139:23–24:

> *Search me, O God, and know my heart! Try me and know my thoughts! And see if there be any grievous way in me, and lead me in the way everlasting!*

Commentary, Part One:

"Will you do me the honor of becoming my wife?"

On our engagement night, my husband boiled lobster tails and served a romantic dinner for two. After we enjoyed his home-cooked meal, he knelt on one knee and proposed. A little flustered, I happily accepted. On our wedding day, I agreed to leave behind my old life, cleave to the new, and bless my husband until death parts us.

Biblically speaking, marriage is a picture of Christ and His church — you and me. Christ chose us. We did not choose Him. Because God is spirit, we have a spiritual connection and unity with God through Christ, as we accept His proposal, receive Him into our hearts, and come to know His heart more fully.

To understand even a glimpse of what we can experience with God is a beautiful purpose He has established for us here on earth. That is true intimacy and fulfillment in His presence. David experienced this under the old covenant. Imagine how much more we can enjoy God's presence under the new covenant.

Consider the Tabernacle in the Old Testament, where God allowed the people of Israel to worship only in the Tabernacle's outer courts. God reserved the innermost chamber, the Holy of Holies, where He resided, for the high priest to bring a sin offering once a year. Since sin is not compatible with God's holiness, the Israelites could not pass through that second veil and live (see Hebrews 9:6–7 and Exodus 26:33).

Yet upon Christ's death and resurrection, the veil between the Holy Place and the Holy of Holies was torn, inviting us into the innermost chamber of God's heart, through Christ (see Hebrews 9:11). Do you hear what this means?

We are no longer meant to worship in the outer room of God's presence, nor adore Him from afar. We are meant to draw near His heart and commune with Him. God has called us beyond the veil into the Holy of Holies, God's dwelling place. He has called us into His presence to make our home in Him (see Hebrews 10:19–20 and Leviticus 16).

Here, He is not just God to us, He is *our* God.

Consider with me three ways God invites us into a covenant relationship with Him through Christ:

Release

To hold fast or cling to God, as Scripture commands us to do with our spouses (Gen. 2:24), we must let go of everything that hinders our grip. God intends for us to leave behind our former life to cling to the new in Him. To do that we must throw off the sin that entangles us (Heb. 12:1). It is vital to come to our Bridegroom vulnerable and willing to walk through pain, grief, mourning, and longing with Him.

Cling

Clinging to God in the secret place of His heart, that inner chamber, is to press in as we allow His Spirit to pour in so that nothing can stand between our vows. It is closing the door to all distractions so intimate fellowship can permeate our hearts. It is seeking God for direction in private and on the go, moment by moment. It is gaining strength in His presence as we wait on Him.

Submit

Like the woman who conceives and gives birth at the proper time, we must wait on the Lord. We must listen to His voice and wait for His leading. We often rush ahead with our agendas directly into a space of contention. In a mature marriage, we learn to walk together, to submit one to another, and to sacrifice for the sake of the other. From conception to the time of birthing a new life, to wait is to hope.

It is a time to prepare with splendid anticipation.

It is to trust God's perfect timing.

It is to allow God to birth little miracles in our lives.

To wait on the Lord is to wait for His return with joyful expectancy.

When David experienced deep satisfaction in God, resulting in praise, he vowed never to let that go. He professed to press in, cling to God, and bless Him all the days of his life.

Questions

Read Psalm 27:1–8 (in the NKJV). Recall the one *thing* David desires of

God (v. 4).

When we seek God's presence, where does He hide us in times of trouble (v. 5, see also Psalm 31:19–20)?

The NKJV describes the "covering of the tent" in verse 5 as the "secret place of the tabernacle." This is a stunning picture of God hiding us in His holy dwelling, the Most Holy Place. If God hides us where no man could dare step foot and live, then whom shall we fear (v. 1) when God places us there?

What reason does David give for praising God (v. 6)?

If the secret place of God's presence is how we cling to God for strength and protection, what is the door into this intimate space (v. 7–8)?

Where is "the secret of God's tabernacle" today (see 1 Corinthians 3:16)?

How do the following verses relate to the concept of cleaving (strength in attachment) as one?

Song of Songs 6:3

John 15:4

Prior to the wilderness, what did David leave behind? What promises did he look forward to?

Christ is constant. He chose you before the foundation of the world (Eph. 1:4). Through His sacrifice and the new covenant, Christ cleaves to you. This means He promises to always be with you and never let you go. The question is, will you press in and cleave to Him?

What do you need to leave behind to press in and cleave to Christ today?

Heavenly Father, *You are constant. You are the same yesterday, today, and forever. Thank You for choosing me before the beginning of time. Thank You for Your purpose, plan, and presence in my life. Reveal anything that may be hindering me from a deeper relationship with You. Help me to release any bitterness, anger, or grudge so I may freely cleave to You in the secret place of Your heart. In Jesus' name, amen.*

> *Therefore a man shall leave his father and mother and hold fast to his wife, and the two shall become one flesh. This mystery is profound, and I am saying that it refers to Christ and the church.*
> Ephesians 5:31–32

Day Three
Under the Shadow

Check Your Posture: Open your hands and heart, and pray Psalm 139:23–24:

> *Search me, O God, and know my heart! Try me and know my thoughts! And see if there be any grievous way in me, and lead me in the way everlasting!*

Soak, Scripture, and Scribble

Soak: search for and listen to the song "Psalm 91 (On Eagles' Wings)" by Shane and Shane, while resting in God's presence.

Going deeper: Consider how God may be prompting your posture in His presence, as you listen.

(Soak)

Scripture Focus: Psalm 91:1, Song of Songs 2:3

Consider Psalm 91:1 in the NKJV: *He who dwells in the secret place of the Most High shall abide under the shadow of the Almighty.*

The terms in Psalm 91:1 are rich with meaning: dwells, secret place, abide, and under the shadow of…

To dwell in the secret place of the Almighty is to enter the innermost chamber of God's heart. It is to grow deep roots and remain (or abide) in that safe place. It is not an occasional place we visit, but the place we live. God's heart, our home.

The result of this sweet communion is God's full protection. Under His shadow, He securely arms us for battle. Because He is our defense, no arrow can harm us.

To be under any shadow implies extreme nearness, closely adhering and remaining in stride with the object's constant presence.

Under the shadow of the Almighty is where we find our strength and soar through every battle.

Although David proved to be a courageous warrior, he looked to God as the strength of his life. Because he abided in the Almighty, he believed in the promise that God would protect and give him victory over his enemy.

We are not immune to physical struggles, but God protects us against spiritual forces, for that is the true battle we face. (Eph. 6:12) This comforts me immensely. Does it comfort you?

Questions

Read Song of Solomon 2:3. The maiden (representing God's people) enjoys the presence of her beloved (representing Jesus). Where does this verse say she sits down?

Do you think "sat down" implies a quick visit or an intentional settling-in to stay?

One source describes the maiden as likely being sun-scorched with leathery skin. How do you think the maiden feels in the presence of her beloved, where a tree shades her from the grueling hot sun? Write about your ideas.

Scribble: Consider yourself as the maiden in Song of Solomon 2:3, delighting in the security of your Beloved's presence. Write about this experience. What would you say? How would you feel? What words would you long to hear? Add this to your confession. Alternately, draw this scene.

"Those who commune with God are safe with Him; no evil can reach them, for the outstretched wings of his power and love cover them from all harm. This protection is constant—they abide under it, and it is all-sufficient, for it is the shadow of the Almighty, whose omnipotence will surely screen them from all attack."[25]

Charles Spurgeon, *The Treasury of David*

Heavenly Father, *You are my refuge and dwelling place. You shade me under the protective wings of Your Almighty presence. You cause me to soar like on eagles' wings when I remain near You. Thank You for covering me with Your power. Help me always remember that You are the strength of my life, and in You is where I discover true victory. In Jesus' name, amen.*

As an apple tree among the trees of the forest, so is my beloved among the young men. With great delight, I sat in his shadow, and his fruit was sweet to my taste.

Song of Solomon 2:3

---

[25] Spurgeon, Charles. *The Treasury of David: The Complete Seven Volumes, Vol. 3*, E-book Ed., 2012, pp.2822.

Day Four
Learning to Depend Fully on God
Upheld by God's Power

Check Your Posture: Open your hands and heart, and pray Psalm 139:23–24:

> *Search me, O God, and know my heart! Try me and know my thoughts! And see if there be any grievous way in me, and lead me in the way everlasting!*

Commentary, Part Two:

After twenty years of marriage, my love for my husband and trust in our relationship have grown stronger. This has occurred as we have matured beyond butterflies and blissful experiences. When we met, being together felt easy. We desired to be continually in each other's presence. After we married, we let go of feelings as our guide and chose to cleave to one another in good and hard times.

Cleaving to God is like this. It is not an occasional date. We choose to trust Him through good and tough times—for better or worse, for richer or poorer, in sickness and health. The result is His promise to uphold us.

When Jesus walked the earth, He was fully human, putting aside His glorified life. Yet He refused to allow His life on earth to be anything but in obedience to God the Father. He prayed in secluded spaces incessantly. He prayed, then taught the crowds; prayed, then performed miracles; prayed, then bore the weight of our sin upon the cross. Jesus' intimacy with the Father strengthened Him for each assignment leading up to His ultimate purpose. We cannot separate Christ's impassioned prayer from His miraculous mission on earth. Prayer and power go hand in hand like the glue that adheres our lives to Christ when we remain connected to Him.

Adhering to Christ does not guarantee our comfort. On the contrary, it will likely bring us to challenging places. Jesus' prayer with the Father also brought Him to hard places like the wilderness where the devil tempted Him. Yet Jesus' trust in the Father empowered Him to confront difficult people and challenging circumstances.

We see this also with David in the wilderness of Judah. Prayer, meditation, and praise reflect his trust in God, empowering him to face and overcome his most difficult circumstances.

When God's right hand upholds us, His power sustains us. God does not uphold us because we do good things, pray at certain times, or check items off the list that make us feel in control and spiritually safe. God upholds us when we take the wild ride of abiding in Christ and going where He leads. He holds us close as our life source and sustains us in times of trouble.

Our quiet time with God in the secret place of His heart may not secure continual comfort. But it does secure His promise to always be with us, to empower us in our anointing, and to shine His light through us in the darkest places.

Questions

Read Acts 16:25–33. Where are Paul and Silas?

What happened when Paul and Silas prayed and sang hymns of praise to God (v. 25)?

What do you think caused this earthquake?

How did the jailer respond (v. 27)?

Under Roman law, if a jailer let a prisoner escape, he received the prisoner's sentence. How did Paul show loving-kindness to the jailer (v. 28)?

How did the jailer respond (v. 29)?

What was the outcome of what started in a jail cell (v. 31-34)?

Our prayers and praise are meant to resound, raising the roof of our circumstances when we fully trust and believe God is able. This empowers us to pour out blessings and power onto those around us.

Heavenly Father, *Your plans for me are wonderful. You not only love me, but You have planned a partnership with me from the beginning. Thank You for the blessing of Your Spirit which empowers me to bless others through my gifts. Please help me to trust that in You, when I am weak, then I am strong. In Jesus' name, amen.*

For the sake of Christ, then, I am content with weakness, insults, hardships, persecutions, and calamities. For when I am weak, then I am strong.

2 Corinthians 12:10

Day Five
Strength in the Wilderness

Check Your Posture: Open your hands and heart, and pray Psalm 139:23–24:

> *Search me, O God, and know my heart! Try me and know my thoughts! And see if there be any grievous way in me, and lead me in the way everlasting!*

Ponder and Personalized Practice

> *Then he showed me a river of the water of life, clear as crystal, coming from the throne of God and of the Lamb, in the middle of its street. On either side of the river was the tree of life, bearing twelve kinds of fruit, yielding its fruit every month; and the leaves of the tree were for the healing of the nations.*
>
> Revelation 22:1–2 (NASB)

Where water exists, so does life. This is true spiritually for us. Where the Holy Spirit resides, and as we abide in Christ, we produce life-giving fruit. Though the wilderness can feel like a desert—lonely and dry—consider, too, the wilderness serves as a reminder to drop our agendas and allow God to draw us back to Himself, our life source.

When we feel stuck in the muck of our wilderness or valley, we only need to turn toward God. What we don't always recognize, but can trust God for, is the groundwater nourishing our roots in times of longing and waiting. He remains ever-present if only we turn and keep our eyes fixed on Him.

God Himself is the promise that remains constant. He is the promise David clung to in the wilderness, giving him strength and resolve. He is the promise we are assured of today.

Ponder: As we close this week, what is Jesus revealing to your heart personally?

Practice: Find a secluded space and practice sitting in silence before the Lord. If you feel the to-dos of your day creeping in, write that list down then set it aside. Promise yourself you will get back to it. Ask God in the silence what He wants to speak to your heart. Have a journal handy for when His words come. Be ready to receive and not analyze. If God feels silent, trust He is there and pay attention throughout your weekend. As you listen, ask God to direct you to Scripture that can affirm His words, and highlight those passages.

Dear Heavenly Father, *You are a good Father. You desire beautiful things for me. You desire connection and to offer me Your abundance. Thank You for Your presence even when I do not feel You are near. Regardless of my feelings, may I turn to You and seek Your face; may I cleave to You as though my strength depends on it – always. In Jesus' name, amen.*

> *For all the promises of God find their Yes in him. That is why it is through him that we utter our Amen to God for his glory.*
> 2 Corinthians 1:20

Scripture Informed Revelation

Beloved,

Your weathered heart and the scars you bear are beautiful to Me. Do not hide your wounds. Do not hide your face from Me. Let Me see your weary eyes. I want to hear your voice. Let Me adorn you. I long to hold you and to heal you.

Remember Me, your first love. Remember how I wooed your heart to Mine? Remember how we danced together and laughed out loud? Remember the joy that spilled over and the hope that consumed you?

Return to Me. Let us discover joy in our intimacy. I'm crazy about you, My love. You are altogether beautiful to Me.

Song of Songs 1:5, 15, 4:1-15
Hosea 2:14-23

Week Six

The Posture of Victory

"Satan has no authority or power over you except what you yield to him when you are deceived into believing his lies."[26]
Victory Over Darkness, Neil. T. Anderson

---

[26] Anderson, Neil. T. *Victory Over Darkness: Realizing the Power of Your Identity in Christ*. Bethany House Publishers, Bloomington, Minnesota, 2012, pp.161.

Day One
Confidently Proclaim Victory

Check Your Posture: Open your hands and heart, and pray Psalm 139:23–24:

> *Search me, O God, and know my heart! Try me and know my thoughts! And see if there be any grievous way in me, and lead me in the way everlasting!*

Devotional
Defeat Is a Feeling

> *But those who seek to destroy my life shall go down into the depths of the earth; they shall be given over to the power of the sword; they shall be a portion for jackals. But the king shall rejoice in God; all who swear by him shall exult, for the mouth of liars will be stopped.*
>
> Psalm 63:9–11

Defeat is a feeling, not our reality unless we allow it to be.

"Why, God? Why didn't You shout Your truth louder?" It was the first question I asked God after believing a lie that left me feeling beaten down and weary. I soon realized, however, that is not how God operates. His character is consistent, and it is up to me to tune into His voice. I can listen to lies or wisely seek the truth. David chose the latter.

Saul knew that God had anointed David to be the next king of Israel, and his jealousy drove him to destroy David. But David knew he had not wronged Saul, so there was nothing to rectify. God was on his side.

In driving David away from the temple, Saul's army attempted to drive him away from God, David's source of power and strength. Not only were they in pursuit of destroying David and his anointing as king, but they were also in pursuit of destroying his soul (mental, spiritual, and physical faculties). This is how the enemy operates. He'll drive us to a place of physical weariness, then attack our mind and worth. He will resort to scorn, mockery, and schemes if he can't distract, discourage, or intimidate us. He will stop at nothing. Yet David's enemies could not break down David's mind or spiritual strength. David knew whom to turn to.

In the wilderness, David clung to God for His protection and praised Him for His favor. Trust was primary to David's countenance. His confidence was secure. He earnestly sought after God's truth. In doing so, he confidently proclaimed victory over his enemies. Even more profound was his proclamation of his advancement in his anointing. By faith, David rejoiced in who God said he was before David ever reigned as king.

The truth is, with God, the enemy has no power. The lies will be stopped!

David endured the enemy's pursuit for about ten years in the physical realm. The attack was real, and it grieved David. Yet the enemy had no power over the spiritual realm, which protected David's mind and strengthened his faith. David's deep communion with God caused him to trust God to deal with his enemies in His time and way. God is just. If He is for us, who can be against us (Rom. 8:31)?

Do not only command the lies swirling in your head to stop. The lies will stop when we humbly acknowledge God as *our* God, seek Him first, remember His promises, meditate on His Word, and praise Him as our proper response to His loving-kindness. In this repeated posture, we can confidently call out lies and proclaim victory in our lives and anointing.

Eventually, the Philistines killed Saul in a battle, and later David stepped into his anointing as king over all of Israel. And yet, there were times when David did not depend on God as deeply as he had in the wilderness. Trust tends to be less when we prosper more. Yet because of his intimate relationship with God, David knew who to turn to in his wilderness moments. We must, too. Will you turn to God and trust Him to deal with your burdens in His time and way?

Defeat is only our reality when we accept a lie as our truth.

For Further Application: Write about the time you decided to put your trust in Jesus. If you have grown up in a Christian home, consider the turning point for you, when you truly made your faith your own. How did that change your daily pursuit of an intimate relationship with Jesus?

Heavenly Father, You are victorious. Because You defeated death on the cross and through your resurrection, I can fight my battles from a place of victory. You go before me and promise that I only need to stand firm and allow You to work in and through me. Thank You for the victory You have secured in my life. Help me to trust you with my whole heart. In Jesus' name, amen.

> *So Jesus said to the Jews who had believed him, "If you abide in my word, you are truly my disciples, and you will know the truth, and the truth will set you free.*
>
> John 8:31-32

Day Two
Breaking Generational Cycles
Anointing

Check Your Posture: Open your hands and heart, and pray Psalm 139:23–24:
Search me, O God, and know my heart! Try me and know my thoughts! And see if there be any grievous way in me, and lead me in the way everlasting!

Commentary, Part One:

When we run from our pain, we run from God.

I used to run from anything that made me feel vulnerable. It manifested itself as an eating disorder in my twenties that I battled for seven long years. I can easily write about it now, but it was a grueling battle that I was not sure I'd win. The enemy thought he had me, but Jesus never left me. My battle was the wilderness where I discovered Christ more deeply and learned how to cling to Him as my strength. It is the place where I found how surrendering to Christ is an essential posture for victory.

The disorder no longer affected me once I was free of it. Once I stopped running from my pain, there was no longer fertile soil for the enemy to taunt me with lies that vulnerability would always be dangerous territory for me. Inviting Jesus into my pain and surrendering control is what saved me.

Trauma entices this survival behavior. The concept is more common in everyday people than you may imagine. Dr. Alison Cook defines trauma simply as unwitnessed pain.[27] When our pain goes unnoticed, it creates a wound. But God is the great healer. He knows our hearts better than anyone. John 10:10 reminds us, "The thief comes only to steal and kill and destroy. I came that they may have life and have it abundantly." We are not meant to remain stuck in our pain but to live life abundantly in our God-given anointing.

Lies do not control me how they used to, but it has been a process. Healing continues through cultivating fertile soil for truth to grow deep roots and bear the fruit of our faith by surrendering to Jesus daily. With ongoing surrender, the whispers of truth will resonate over the shouts of a lie until it silences the lies. This is the promise on the last day when Jesus returns. Until that day, a battle for our souls wages. We must fight by standing our ground, finding safe people to support us, and allowing God to uphold us in battle. We will have to cling to Jesus as our defender and

---

[27] https://www.dralisoncook.com/blog/what-are-the-effects-of-trauma

protector, and we will have to take risks as we step into our anointing. Like David, we can do this with confidence amidst any circumstance.

In the wilderness of Judah, David announced that "those who seek to destroy my life shall go down into the depths of the earth" (Ps. 63:9). He was referring to those Israelites who opposed God's purposes by seeking to destroy him—God's faithful servant. Not just his life, but his soul. For us, the true enemy will be the powers of this world and the spiritual forces of evil in the heavenly realms (Eph. 6:12). They will show up in our thoughts and habits. They will show up generation after generation until we determine, "No more!"

Furthermore, David prophesied that his enemies would not only *be given over to the power of the sword,* but *they would be a portion for the jackals.* This is a profound statement that only a deep confidence and trust in God's promises can speak of. The reason is that jackals are scavengers that come and finish off a carcass that the birds and large beasts leave behind, leaving no trace of it. In the end, there will be no trace of the enemy. The lies and all evidence of them will be stopped (Ps. 63:11).

If acknowledging God through prayer and meditation is the doorway to God's heart, then acknowledging our unwelcome feelings opens the door for God to enter ours. There He will work out healing and gently remind us of His truth. Let us not only seek to enter the secret place of God's heart through prayer and meditation on Him but also allow God to enter our hearts through honesty and vulnerability with Him. Bring Him your deepest cares, worries, and fears. Bring Him your sorrows and shame. He already knows your struggle. He is waiting.

When we allow this two-way relationship with our God, we will walk out of that intimate space stronger and more resilient in the power of the Holy Spirit. We will be ready to make noise for the kingdom of Heaven. We will be prepared to take that next step in our anointing. We will be equipped to fight from a place of healing and victory. In addition, God will empower us to break generational cycles of defeat and leave a legacy of victory for future generations.

It is time to stop running from our doubts. It is time to acknowledge our pain even if no one else has. It is time to find trusted people and heal those wounds. It is time to put ourselves out there, take risks, make mistakes, be willing to fail, and learn. Take the risks God is whispering into your heart and recognize that you are never alone.

It will not happen overnight. Yet we will gain resilience with time—one step in trust, one step in vulnerability, and one step closer to God's heart at a time. We are not running anymore. We are not running from our pain. We are not running from the risks God is calling us to. *We are inviting Jesus into them.*

This is our posture for victory.

What struggle do you need to invite Jesus into today?

Questions

Another way to define the term "anointed" is "prepared and empowered for God's service."

Read Isaiah 45:1-7. Cyrus was a pagan king that God anointed to fulfill His purposes. As God's anointed, how is God using Cyrus as His instrument (v. 1)?

What victories does God promise (v. 2-3)?

Who is responsible for these victories?

If God's purposes stand behind one's anointing, how should we manage the discouragement of circumstances that appear to go against His promises?

Read Isaiah 61:1-7. Isaiah prophesies the empowerment of the Messiah's ministry in this passage. What are the purposes God has anointed the Messiah to do (v. 1-3)?

Within the context of the Messiah's purpose, how are the people anointed to partner with Him (v. 4–7)?

If God anointed Jesus to fulfill His purposes, how much more do we need God's anointing to participate in fulfilling His purposes for our lives?

Read 1 John 2:20–27. What does John say is the result of one's anointing (v. 20–22)?

According to verses 24–27, when God anoints us, the anointing we receive abides (or lives) *within us*. We must tap into our anointing and allow God's Spirit to teach us how to live *in Christ*.

Consider what it means to live in this two-way relationship with Christ.

What is the promise of this relationship?

Read 2 Corinthians 1:20–22. Paul echoes the promise of anointing for all believers in Christ. Describe this promise in your own words.

Consider how God has anointed you to partner with Him in His Kingdom work.

Dear Heavenly Father, *You are our Healer and Great Physician. You hold all things together. You make all things new. You are trustworthy. Thank*

You for residing in the vulnerable places of my heart and calling me out into the light of Your glory. Help me to pursue this two-way relationship with You so that You may have Your way in me. In Jesus' name, amen.

> *No, in all these things we are more than conquerors through him who loved us.*
>
> Romans 8:37

Day Three
Crowns of Victory

Check Your Posture: Open your hands and heart, and pray Psalm 139:23–24:

> *Search me, O God, and know my heart! Try me and know my thoughts! And see if there be any grievous way in me, and lead me in the way everlasting!*

Soak, Scripture, Scribble

Soak: Search and listen to the song "We Fall Down" by Chris Tomlin (also covered by Nichole Nordeman) while resting in God's presence.

Alternately: listen to "Revelation Song."

Going deeper: Consider a humble position at Jesus' feet, as you listen.

(Soak)

Scripture Focus: Revelation 4

When we understand that Jesus is worthy to receive all glory, honor, and praise, we will understand the power and responsibility of our anointing. As we walk in our anointing, God gives us the power to break generational cycles and leave a legacy of victory. Then on that glorious day when we meet Jesus, we will cast our crowns at His feet, worshiping and acknowledging that our victories were all because of Him. Think about that. Our victories are because of His victory!

This changes how I walk in my anointing. It's not about me or anyone but Jesus. Does this change your perspective?

Questions

Read Revelation 4. John authored the book of Revelation on the island of Patmos, where he experienced a heavenly vision. What does he see in heaven (v. 2)?

What is surrounding the throne? What does it represent (v. 3)?

How does this biblical symbol in verse 3 reveal God's character (Gen. 9:11–

17)? How does it connect to the "throne of grace" in Hebrews 4:16?

Describe what the crowns in verses 10–11 represent for you and me.

Scribble: Imagine the day you will cast your crowns at Jesus' feet, giving all glory, honor, and praise to Him. What victories do you envision your crowns represent? Consider the small, humble, and insignificant ways only God sees and the risks that lead to the more obvious ways. How will these crowns impact future generations? Proclaim the advancement of God's anointing on your life for future generations. Write about this to conclude your confession. Alternately, sketch those crowns and what they represent at Jesus's feet as a reminder of where your victory comes from.

"The crowns mentioned in Revelation 4:10 are the *Stephanos* crowns, the crowns of victory, not royalty."[28]

David Guzik

Oh God, I praise You because You are worthy of all praise. Holy, holy,

---

[28] Guzik, David. "Study Guide for Revelation 4." Blue Letter Bible. 6/2022. Web. 8 June, 2023. <https://www.blueletterbible.org/comm/guzik_david/study-guide/revelation/revelation-4.cfm>.

holy are You. You are limited only by Your promises. How good You are to fulfill each of them for Your ultimate glory. From the beginning of time to the end, You are worthy. Lord, may all I do be for and because of You. May I lay my crowns at Your feet on that glorious day. Until then, help me to lean in and trust You through the wilderness. Surely this is where You will meet me. In Jesus' name, amen.

> They cast their crowns before the throne, saying, "Worthy are you, our
> Lord and God, to receive glory and honor and power, for you created
> all things, and by your will they existed and were created."
> Revelation 4:10b-11

Day Four
Breaking Generational Cycles
How Liars Are Silenced

Check Your Posture: Open your hands and heart, and pray Psalm 139:23–24:

> *Search me, O God, and know my heart! Try me and know my thoughts! And see if there be any grievous way in me, and lead me in the way everlasting!*

Commentary, Part Two:

Fear is a liar and a thief.

The year 2020 was a bizarre time. We are still feeling the aftermath of the pandemic. Part of the aftermath is positive, such as appreciating the need to slow down and utilizing virtual options more. Yet fear stole from too many lives.

After three months of quarantine, our family took the first opportunity to travel to Washington and visit my in-laws and the children's grandparents. Everyone craved the outdoors one afternoon, so we gathered our masks and ventured out for a hike. Along our hike, we passed numerous hikers geared up in their hiking shoes and masks. Yet what we witnessed was far from camaraderie. We did not pass cautious civilians; we passed fearful strangers who stopped and turned their backs to us as we passed. We passed people who chose not to make eye contact with us or notice the smile in our eyes. People who could not return the kind gesture of a simple "hello."

Fear isolates us and causes us to act inhumanly. The true pandemic was not COVID-19, it was fear sweeping nationwide. People became depleted of the abundant life that Jesus offered us in John 10:10. They became victims of the thief who came to steal, kill, and destroy.

Fear is ugly. It is a liar and will rob us of an abundant life.

Recall how David dealt with an even greater assault on his life. He rejoiced. This came with a process of acknowledging his fear, grief, and longing. As a result, he rejoiced. He rejoiced amidst his enemies' pursuit of him. He rejoiced in the promise of God's anointing, though he had not yet attained it. David rejoiced because he trusted God. Jesus' abundance is not conditional to our circumstances. The abundance Jesus promises us comes amidst our circumstances.

David announced that all who swear by God will exult (Ps. 63:11). In other words, they will feel triumphant elation. The word "swear" in

Hebrew is *saba*, meaning the cardinal number seven, or to be complete.[29] It is like declaring God seven times. When we swear by God, we place our complete confidence in Him. David had not yet advanced in his anointing as king when he proclaimed victory, but like a night watchman does not doubt the morning will come, David anticipated the promise with complete assurance. We have reason to praise and progress when we know with certainty the victory is ours, even in trials or a time of wait. This is how we stop the mouths of liars.

Friend, we will either trust God or believe lies. When we believe lies, we inadvertently declare them over ourselves and our loved ones. We repeat generational cycles that we desperately need to break. Fear is a liar that takes control if we allow it.

Verse 11 shows us the difference between the mouth that finds reason to praise and the mouth that spews lies. One will continue forever, and the other will stop.

On that day of Christ's second coming, the lies will finally stop, and victory will have the final say. Until that day, we have the tools to stop the lies before they even start. We know the posture of victory!

If you struggle with speaking God's truth over your life and bringing out God's best in others, know it will take practice, allowing for growth and maturity in your faith. Spiritual maturity is an ongoing process for all of us. No one person has arrived on this side of heaven. The more you are willing to heal your earthly wounds, the more you will spiritually mature in your faith. Bring your struggle to Jesus and invite Him into it. Offer a humble and contrite heart. Be vulnerable, ready to listen, and prepared to take one step of obedience. Be ready. It is time to kick defeat to the curb.

What one step of obedience is Christ asking you to take today?

Questions

Read Ephesians 6:10–17. There are two vital postures to standing against the enemy stated in verses 10–11. What are they (also see 1 Samuel 30:6)?

Do you see this as an active or passive posture? How so?

[29] "H7650 - šāba' - Strong's Hebrew Lexicon (kjv)." Blue Letter Bible. Web. 12 June, 2023. <https://www.blueletterbible.org/lexicon/h7650/kjv/wlc/0-1/>.

Read Isaiah 59:14–21. According to verse 17, who else uses the armor Paul instructs us to put on? To whom does the armor belong?

We need this armor to fight. Either we can put it on and fight for God, or He will. One way or another, He will get the job done. How are we ensured victory when we partner with God (Rom. 8:37)?

God's strength and armor allow us to stand against the enemy's schemes. Is God's strength automatic when we become Christians? What is our responsibility in the battle?

When we stand firm, even as we go, what does Ephesians 6:18 say to do?

What:

When:

How:

Read James 4:6–10. According to verse 6, what does God offer for the battle? To whom?

According to verse 7, what must we do to receive it? Resist means stand against. How does this allow us to stand against the devil?

What is the promise when we draw near God (v.8)?

Read Revelation 20:1–15. According to verses 2 and 3, who is responsible for binding the devil and shutting him up?

According to Revelation 20:12, by God's grace, He wrote us into the Book of Life, but those who do not receive Him will be blotted out (also see Exodus 32:32). What will those names that are not found in the Book of Life be judged upon?

Are well-intended, good works enough to measure up to God's holiness outside of His grace?

What does God's grace mean to you right now?

Heavenly Father, *although I see life in snapshots, You hold the big picture. How profound You are. You are a loving God. You do not give me a spirit of fear, but of power, love, and self-control (2 Tim. 1:7). Thank You for Your grace that allows me to draw near to You and resist the devil. Help me to remember that the devil is powerless over me unless I allow him access. In You, sin and death, fear and doubt cannot hold me captive. I am free to live and love abundantly, in You! In Jesus' name, amen.*

> *For God gave us a spirit not of fear but of power and love and self-control.*
>
> 2 Timothy 1:7

Day Five
Victory through the Wilderness

Check Your Posture: Open your hands and heart, and pray Psalm 139:23–24:

Search me, O God, and know my heart! Try me and know my thoughts! And see if there be any grievous way in me, and lead me in the way everlasting!

Ponder and Personalized Practice

Blessed are the poor in spirit, for theirs is the kingdom of heaven.

Matthew 5:3

The foundation for living victoriously is the fertile soil of true humility.

In the above beatitude, Jesus is not suggesting that those who strive to be humble will receive the kingdom of heaven. He is not advising that we conjure up this spirit on our own. Nor is He suggesting that this is already the condition of a Christian's heart. He is announcing that those who understand that we become humble only by God's work and grace will also understand the gospel and its outcome.

No matter how hard we try, we are never sufficiently humble in and of ourselves. We are only sufficiently humble in Christ. This requires constantly leaning in and surrendering to His way, moment by moment, day by day.

This kind of humility will cause us to bloom and burst with the sweet aroma of Christ. It will always bring out the best in us.

It takes humility to allow God to be our healer and to allow Christ's sacrifice to mend our broken pieces. It takes humility to discover our identity in Christ and cling to Him like we desperately need Him. It takes humility to go where God leads. You may be thinking this also takes courage. It does. But courage is born of humility. Humility is foundational to a victorious life in Christ.

Whether at the top or the bottom rung, whether placed first or last, we attain true humility by allowing God to be all.

As with David in the wilderness of Judah, when we fix our eyes on Christ, the enemy cannot break down our minds or steal our spiritual strength.

This brings us full circle in our study. Our posture begins and ends with humility. As we close this week, consider how David's humble posture in his anointing as King impacted God's ultimate plan for salvation.

What impact can your obedience and complete trust in God have on the salvation of your future heritage?

Ponder: God has anointed you to fulfill His calling on your life. What dream or desire has He placed on your heart? Be bold. Remember David called himself king before he ever reigned as king. What is one thing you can do today to respond to God's call?

Practice: Catch the sunrise one morning. Notice how you never doubted the sun would rise. No matter what is happening in your life or this world, the sun faithfully and miraculously rises and sets. Rest assured that you can trust God's promises over you as sure as the sunrise. As you consider its beauty and promise, thank God for His faithfulness.

"In this view it is of inconceivable importance that we should have right thoughts of what Christ is, of what really constitutes Him the Christ, and specially of what may be counted His chief characteristic, the root and essence of all His character as our Redeemer. There can be but one answer: it is His humility."[30]

Andrew Murray, *Humility*

Lord, You overwhelm me in the best way. Your beauty is the one thing I seek. Thank You for Your grace and immeasurable love. I speak authority over generational bondage, and healing throughout my family heritage, in Jesus' name. I declare life over my children and family. The enemy has no power over my life. You have the final say. Your victory begins with me today. In Jesus' name, amen.

> And being found in human form, he humbled himself by becoming obedient to the point of death, even death of a cross. Therefore, God elevated him to the place of highest honor and gave him the name above all other names, so that at the name of Jesus every knee should bow, in heaven and on earth and under the earth, and every tongue confess that Jesus Christ is Lord, to the glory of God the Father.
>
> Philippians 2:8-11

---

[30] Murray, Andrew. *Humility*. Publishing Group, Nashville, Tennessee, 2017, pp.14.

Scripture Informed Revelation

Beloved,

You are victorious in Me and Me alone.

Know there is an enemy on your heels who is stronger than you. He is the one out to destroy your soul. Do you see that you cannot win the war he wages against you, or this battle, on your own? Can you see you are powerless against your enemy without Me? Resist the devil by turning to Me.

I will reach out and take hold of you. I will rescue you from the suffocating waters of your enemy's grip. I will bring you to a safe and spacious place. I will deliver you because I delight in you.

You must trust what I can do through you because of what I have done for you. My Son determines your victory. Lean in, abide, and cling to Me.

I would stop at nothing to save you from the destruction of the enemy because I love you. Trust in Me.

1 Corinthians 15:57
1 John 5:4
John 16:33
John 15:4
James 4:7
Isaiah 41:13
Psalm 18:19
John 14:12
John 3:16
Proverbs 3:5

Conclusion

Friend, we have been together for six weeks now and I am guessing it has been encouraging and challenging. Thank you for taking this journey with me and seeing it through. You are truly courageous and dear to God's heart. Although this study has ended, this is not the endpoint. Like a young adult with the world before her and ready to spread her wings, this is the launching point. God has so much more in store for you. Today is meant to launch you into a life clinging to Christ like David did, as you victoriously walk out your God-given anointing. You will not do that perfectly. Neither did David. But you know the One you can continually turn to and cling to.

If it takes you the rest of your earthly life, I want you to begin breaking the cycles of defeat. I will be right here alongside you, slaying my own. We will be victorious together, allowing God to be our all-in-all.

Friend, I deeply care about you. We may not personally know each other yet, but I am confident that together we will be casting our crowns at Jesus' feet one day, giving Him all glory, honor, and praise for every one of our victories. I look forward to that day. Until then, I am cheering you on.

Remember when opposition pursues, pursue God.

Do not wait. The time is now. Pursue Him today.

The next generation is at stake!

Let us close by proclaiming this statement as our declaration of victory:

I am (your name), a child of the Most High, God. I have chosen and called to partner with Christ in building the kingdom of heaven through the gift of (your God-given gifts or anointing), and through the power of the Holy Spirit. I intend to break generational strongholds of defeat by allowing Jesus into my struggles and pain and to walk out healing from a place of victory. I commit to remaining in Christ as I pursue Him wholeheartedly on the front lines of my battles. I commit to always acknowledging God as my God. When I feel afraid, I will seek Him. When I feel anxious, I will remember Him. When I feel tormented by lies or temptation, I will meditate on Him. When I face storms, I will praise Him. When I need strength, I will cling to Him. My posture will remain one of humility and surrender to Christ alone. I will take risks in the areas God is calling me to and has anointed me for. I will trust God's promises and provisions for leaving the next generation a victorious legacy. This is my posture of victory.

God wants to give you the abundant life He has promised you from the beginning, from the inside out. If proclaiming victory falls flat in your life, stop 🤚, check your posture 🙏, and humbly proclaim who God is 👣. This is a great place to start.

Finally, I'd like to part with this final blessing:

> *The LORD bless you and keep you;*
> *the LORD make his face to shine upon you and be gracious to you;*
> *the LORD lift up his countenance upon you and give you peace.*
>
> Numbers 6:24–26

God is crazy about you. You are beautiful and so dearly loved.

Appendix One

Commitment Prayer of Salvation

Dear God,

I recognize my need for a Savior. I admit I am not in right standing with You. I cannot achieve the righteousness required for salvation simply by being good. I need You. I ask for Your forgiveness for where I have missed the mark. The Bible says that if I confess with my mouth that Jesus is Lord and believe in my heart that God raised Him from the dead, I will be saved (Rom. 10:9). Today I confess and believe in my heart that You are the Lord and Savior of my life. Come make Your home in me. In Jesus' name, amen

Recommitment Prayer of Salvation

Dear God,

I surrender all. I recognize that I am nothing without You and everything with You. I need You to be the Lord of my life. I admit that my way is not working. Please forgive me for my stubbornness. I trust that Your ways are good and perfect. Today, I commit not just my life but also my choices to You. Help me to grow in my relationship with You as I trust and obey You completely. Come and dwell in my heart today and every day. In Jesus' name, amen.

Appendix Two

My Declaration of Victory

I am _____, a child of the Most High God. I am called and chosen to partner with Christ in building the Kingdom of Heaven through the gift(s) of _____ and through the power of the Holy Spirit. I will break generational strongholds of defeat by inviting Jesus into my pain and walk in healing from a place of victory.

I commit to remaining in Christ as I pursue Him wholeheartedly on the front lines of my battles. I will acknowledge God as my Lord. When I feel afraid, I will seek Him. When I feel anxious, I will remember Him. When tormented by lies or temptation, I will meditate on His truth. When I face storms, I will praise Him. When I need strength, I will cling to Him.

My posture will be one of humility and surrender to Christ alone. I will take risks in the areas God calls and has anointed me. I will trust God's promises and provisions to leave a victorious legacy for the next generation. This is my declaration of victory.

Appendix Three

Scan the QR Code to retrieve the Posture of Victory Playlist:

Acknowledgments

I am deeply grateful to my Heavenly Father for the way He gracefully opened doors as I dedicated myself to completing this study. I felt God's gentle nudge each step of the way, guiding me on this journey and encouraging me to see this project through to the end with unwavering faith.

I want to thank my family for believing in God's anointing over me, and my wonderful husband for supporting me through this process and encouraging me to "execute."

I want to thank the prayer team and my lovely focus group, who worked through the study in its unedited form and offered me encouragement and feedback.

Thank you, Mt. Zion Ridge Press, for believing in this work and expressing your excitement.

Finally, I want to thank my dear friend, Angie Gilbert, who dedicated her time to proofreading this study as I wrote it. Your commitment was truly a gift to me.

"You have a gift. When you use it, you are the gift."

Angie Gilbert

About the Author

Theresa Miller is adventurous at heart and dedicated to pursuing spiritual, mental, and emotional healing for the betterment of future generations.

Originally from the wooded East, Theresa now resides in the wide-open spaces of Wyoming, nestled near the Big Horn Mountains. She cherishes her role as a wife to Rob and mother to their four children. Weaving words has been her creative outlet since childhood, bringing clarity to life's complexities.

Theresa is the co-author of, *Unexpected Blessings: 40 Days of Discovering God's Best*. She serves in women's ministries as a Bible teacher and a MomCo Mentor in her community. She co-founded Dandelions, Potholes, & Wrinkles and The Sisters on Purpose Podcast with three of her sisters. Theresa encourages women to dig deeper to reach higher in their faith and callings on Instagram @theresammillerauthor, Facebook, her professional website, and the podcast she hosts with her sisters.

Discover free resources, social links, and books on Theresa's Website:

THANK YOU!

Thank you for reading this book from Mt. Zion Ridge Press.

If you enjoyed the experience, learned something, gained a new perspective, or made new friends through story, could you do us a favor and write a review on Goodreads or wherever you bought the book?

Thanks! We and our authors appreciate it.

We invite you to visit our website, MtZionRidgePress.com, and explore other titles in fiction and non-fiction. We always have something coming up that's new and off the beaten path.

And please check out our podcast, **Books on the Ridge,** where we chat with our authors and give them a chance to share what was in their hearts while they wrote their book, as well as fun anecdotes and glimpses into their lives and experiences and the writing process. And we always discuss a very important topic: *Tea!*

You can listen to the podcast on our website or find it at most of the usual places where podcasts are available online. Please subscribe so you don't miss a single episode!

Thanks for reading. We hope you come back soon!